HIDDEN

• LIKE ANNE FRANK •

Fourteen True Stories of Survival

H I D

MARCEL PRINS & PETER HENK STEENHUIS
Translated by Laura Watkinson

DEN

LIKE ANNE FRANK

Scholastic Inc.

Originally published as *Ondergedoken als Anne Frank*, copyright © 2011 by Marcel Prins and Peter Henk Steenhuis

Translation by Laura Watkinson copyright © 2014 by Scholastic Inc.

Arthur A. Levine Books hardcover edition designed by Phil Falco, published by Arthur A. Levine Books, an imprint of Scholastic Inc., April 2014.

ISBN 978-0-545-54364-4

12 11 10 9 8 7 6 5   19 20 21

Printed in the U.S.A.   40
First printing, April 2016

Photographs on pages 44, 46, and 89 © NIOD Institute for War, Genocide, and Holocaust Studies. Photographs on pages 59, 214-221 © Marcel Prins. Photograph on page 73 © archief De Arbeiderspers/Stadsarchief Amsterdam. Photograph on page 87 used with the permission of Herinneringscentrum Kamp Westerbork. Chapter opener maps by Marcel van der Drift. All other photographs are from private collections of the interviewees, and are used with permission.

The text was set in Adobe Garamond, a typeface designed by Robert Slimbach in 1989. The display type was set in Copperplate Gothic, designed by Frederic W. Goudy in 1901.

For my mother, who inspired me to start this project

— M.P.

FOREWORD

This book tells the stories of fourteen people who had to go into hiding during World War II because they were Jewish. Adolf Hitler, the leader of the Nazi Party in Germany, believed the Jews were the cause of all evil in the world. So they had to be destroyed. My mother was considered to be a part of that "evil." But she was one of the lucky ones: She was hidden, and she survived.

At that time — summer 1942 — she was nearly six years old. Even as a little boy, I was curious about the story of her time in hiding. She told me what had happened. The exciting parts and the times when she had been scared or sad made a particularly strong impression on me.

Later, when I started to look into the experiences of other people who went into hiding, I found out that their stories were all very different. And that many of the people who went into hiding had not survived the war, because someone revealed their location or the Nazis found them during raids. About 28,000 Jews were hidden in the Netherlands. Roughly 16,000 survived and 12,000 were caught or betrayed in hiding. The most famous example is, of course, Anne Frank, whose diary has been read by people all over the world.

But what did going into hiding actually involve? Where did you go? How did you know who to trust? How did you find money to pay for your hiding place? What did you do when you were frightened? These are the kinds of questions that I asked men and women who are old now but who were young boys and girls during the war. You can read about their experiences in this book. The first story is my mother's.

There is a website accompanying the book: www.hidden likeannefrank.com. There you can see more photographs, watch short animated clips, and hear a part of each person's story as it was told to me. You can also learn about other young people who went into hiding, whose stories are not included here.

In this book, we've included a map at the beginning of every chapter that shows the places in the Netherlands where that person went into hiding. Sometimes it was only one address, but it was usually several locations. One of the people in this book hid in more than forty-two different places! There is also an interactive map on the website, where you can click on a dot on the map to hear and see the story that happened in that place.

Read, look, and listen!

Marcel Prins

Rita with her mother, Bertha Degen-Groen, c. 1939

THE STARS
HAVE GONE AWAY

RITA DEGEN
Born in Amsterdam on December 25, 1936

In 1939, when I was three years old, my father was called up for the army. The camp was located near the Grebbe Line, which was an important point of defense. My mother and I went there on the train twice to visit him. He was out there with a group of soldiers, all of them in uniform, and I remember thinking how strange they looked. They were living in a large farmhouse. Mom and I were allowed to stay overnight in a separate room. I thought it was kind of fun.

When the war broke out, my father's regiment had to march toward the Grebbeberg, a hill that was in a strategic position. There was heavy fighting, and lots of men were wounded and dying. My father realized it was going badly, so he grabbed his bike and rode back to Amsterdam. He arrived in the middle of the night, without his rifle and his kit bag. He must have gotten rid of them somewhere.

My father always liked to know exactly what was going on, so he found a job with the **Jewish Council**,[1] which had been founded in 1941 on the orders of the Germans to represent the Jewish community in the Netherlands. My father was on guard duty when one of the first groups of Jewish people was transported out of Amsterdam. What he saw made him decide to send me into hiding right away. My parents went into hiding that same week. He had already arranged hiding places for all of us, not just

---

1. **Jewish Council** (German: *Judenrat*): administrative organizations that the German occupiers ordered Jewish communities to set up to manage Jewish affairs. The council had the task of carrying out some of the measures that the Germans imposed on the Jews. Anyone who worked for the Jewish Council was temporarily exempted from deportation. Thousands of people were involved in the work of these organizations.

Many Jewish people resented the council members, particularly the leaders, for following the orders of the occupying Germans, and they thought the exemption from deportation was unfair, but a lot of Jewish Council members secretly tried to help others whenever they had the chance.

for the immediate family but also for his parents and for all of my mother's brothers and sisters. But they never made use of them. "It won't be as bad as all that," they said.

Soon after my parents went into hiding, their house was "Pulsed," or cleared out. The Germans had given Abraham Puls and his company the job of emptying the houses of Jews who had gone into hiding or who had been rounded up during a **raid**.[2] We were lucky: Our neighbors, who were good people, had a key to our house, and they took everything they could carry and hid it for us. After the war, we got back our photographs, a set of cutlery, a figurine, and a clock.

The first address where I went into hiding was in Amsterdam, at my father's boss's house. He was Jewish but his wife was not. **Mixed marriages**[3] of this kind seemed relatively safe at first, but it was still risky for them to take in and hide a Jewish child. It was around this time that I began to realize I was Jewish, without really understanding what that meant.

Before the war, our family had been all kinds of things: vegetarians, followers of holistic healing, and atheists. Of course, we had traditions. We had plenty of them, in fact. We ate matzos at Passover, and my mother would bake *gremsjelies*, a special Passover cake made from matzos, raisins, almonds, and candied citrus peel. We owned a menorah, a candelabrum used in Jewish worship,

---

2. **raid**: a police or army action to find people and take them into custody.
3. **mixed marriage**: usually a marriage between two people of different religious backgrounds or nationalities. In this case, a marriage between a Jew and a non-Jew. Generally, Jews in mixed marriages were not required to report for deportation, and their children did not have to wear stars on their clothing to indicate that they were Jewish. They did, however, have to obey the other rules that the German occupiers had made for Jews.

and we used to light candles. My mother also used a lot of Yiddish expressions, but that was just normal for me.

What was not normal was having to leave kindergarten about three months after the war started. The little boy who lived next door was also Jewish, and the same thing happened to him. So we just went back to playing together again, as we had before we started kindergarten.

I began to get a better understanding of what it meant to be Jewish when my foster parents started discussing my birthday. When I went into hiding, I was five and it was months before my sixth birthday, which I was already looking forward to. My foster father, Walter Lorjé, said, "If anyone asks how old you're going to be on your next birthday, you have to say five. Never tell them you're almost six."

I thought that was awful. I wanted to be a big girl. "Why not?" I asked.

"When you're six," he replied, "you have to wear a **star**."[4]

I knew that you didn't want to have that star on your clothes. My mother had had to wear a star, and it was a nuisance. I was five and I didn't fully understand what it meant to be Jewish, but I could sense that there was something wrong with it. That feeling grew stronger by the week, especially when the raids started and conversations were often about who had been rounded up and who was still around.

The Lorjé family, who had taken me in, had three children. The eldest, Wim, was fifteen. We sometimes used to play together

---

4. **star**: a Star of David on a yellow background with the word *Jood* (Dutch: Jew) in the center. From May 3, 1942, all Jews six years and older had to wear this star on their outer clothes. The star had to be clearly visible and firmly attached, or the person would be punished.

with his toy cars. That always made me so happy, because it meant that I could do something with another person for once. I didn't get to play with friends, saw none of my family, and didn't go to school. I was very eager to learn, but no one taught me anything. Their daughter Marjo had made me terrified, not of the Germans but of beetles, spiders, dirt, and all kinds of other imaginary dangers. I didn't dare to flush the toilet anymore because I thought all kinds of things would come whooshing out of it.

Whenever Aunt Loes, a cousin of Mrs. Lorjé's, came to visit, I had to go out to a nearby playground. Aunt Loes was married to the man who managed the family's stationery store. Mr. Lorjé was Jewish, so the Germans had handed over the management of the store to Aunt Loes's husband. He was called a *Verwalter* in German, an administrator. Aunt Loes often used to visit the house to discuss the stationery store. If I happened to bump into her, I'd been told to say I was Rita Houtman, who lived across the street. I had to go out and stay in the nearby playground until the coast was clear, and then someone would come for me.

But one time it was different. Aunt Loes had said she was coming to visit, so Marjo took me to the playground. As she left, she said, "Aunt Loes won't stay long. You can come home at six." Of course, she should never have said that.

In the playground, there was a slide and a merry-go-round that you had to push yourself. I didn't do that. There were also a couple of swings and a seesaw. But you can't seesaw by yourself, so I didn't do that either. I just sat there with my little pail and shovel in the wet sand of an enormous sandbox. All of the other children had gone to school. I just sat there alone in the playground, which was surrounded by a tall chicken-wire fence. After a while, I began to feel cold and thirsty.

As soon as the church clock struck six, I picked up my pail and shovel and ran home.

The front door was closed, so I rang the bell. Someone upstairs pulled the rope to open the door. There, halfway down the stairs, was Aunt Loes. She looked at me. "And who might you be?"

I knew right away that this wasn't good. "I'm Rita Houtman. I live on the other side of the street. I've just come to see if Mrs. Lorjé has some sugar to spare."

She turned to Mr. Lorjé, who was standing at the top of the stairs, and said, "Hmm, if I didn't know better, I'd think that was Rita Degen." Then she walked past me and out of the house.

Huge panic. My suitcase was packed immediately, and I was taken to stay with someone in **the resistance**[5] that night. The next day, a woman came to pick me up. "Hello," she said, "I'm Aunt Hil. We're taking the train together tomorrow, to Hengelo."

Taking the train to Hengelo. That'd be fun. I hadn't been on a train for ages.

"Hengelo," Aunt Hil told me the next day, "is where Aunt Marie and Uncle Kees live. They're very nice people. And they're really excited about meeting you. They so want you to come and live with them. They have a little baby too, who's not even a year old yet."

It was a long journey, and by the time we reached Hengelo I knew everything I needed to know. I knew what Aunt Marie and

---

5. **the resistance**: organizations carrying out activities against occupying forces, such as helping people go into hiding, printing and distributing underground newspapers, and acts of sabotage.

Uncle Kees looked like and that I was going to be living in a corner house with a garden, and I really believed that they were looking forward to seeing me.

Just before we reached the house, Aunt Hil said to me, "Shall we play a little joke on them? Why don't you sit down with your suitcase on the sidewalk at the front of the house, and I'll go around the back? I'll say to them, 'I have bad news, I'm afraid. Rita couldn't come with me after all.' They'll be really disappointed, of course. And to make it up to them, I'll say that I've brought them a package and it's out front on the sidewalk. They'll go take a look and when they open up the door . . . Surprise!"

I thought it was a great idea. Aunt Hil walked around to the back of the house.

A couple of minutes later, the front door swung open. I could tell that the woman who came to the door was a very nice person. "Oh, Hil!" she said. "You were just teasing me. Rita, how wonderful that you're here! Come in, come in. Your room's all ready. And won't Uncle Kees be pleased when he gets home!"

At the time, I had no idea that Aunt Hil had actually taken me to her sister's house. She didn't have a clue that I was coming, and Aunt Hil had to explain to her first. I had no reason to suspect. The room was beautiful, just as Aunt Hil had said it would be. It wasn't until long after the war that Uncle Kees told me the room had been prepared for any child who might have to go into hiding, and not just for me.

Right from the start, I felt perfectly at home at that second address. I didn't doubt for a moment that I was truly wanted. Aunt Hil, who also stayed for a few days, told Uncle Kees that I was a Christmas baby. "She was born on Christmas Day." They thought that was wonderful. Uncle Kees pointed at their own baby and said, "Wim will be one when you're seven."

That gave me a real shock! When I was almost six, I'd had to say I was going to be five on my next birthday, so now that I was going to be seven, I should be saying I was nearly six. I thought I was always going to have to fib and keep knocking a year off my age or they'd make me wear a star.

"Hey, what's wrong?" asked Uncle Kees, who could see the fear on my face.

"You can't say that. You have to say I'm nearly six."

"Why?"

"If I say that I'll be seven on my next birthday, then I'll have to wear a star."

"You don't have to wear a star at all," said Uncle Kees. "From now on, your name is Rita Fonds. You live here with us. You are our little Rita-pie and our little Rita-pie doesn't wear a star, because no one in our house wears a star."

So now I was one of the Fonds family, and not one of the stars. And then I thought: The stars have gone away. That made me feel so good, even though I didn't know at the time what the stars really meant.

But I still felt like there was something strange about me. I didn't go to school, for example, but had private lessons. They said it was because I hadn't learned anything yet and I had to catch up. I learned how to read and write in no time. I was really eager to learn, because I wanted to read my parents' letters and I wanted to write back. It wasn't because I was really missing them but

Rita with her "brother," Wim, 1944

more because I enjoyed writing. As far as I was concerned, my parents were just snapshots. I had a photograph in my room: They were my mother and father, and I wrote them letters. But it didn't feel real at all. I never worried about how the letters actually reached my parents. Even after I'd caught up with my lessons, I didn't ever go to school in Hengelo. Apparently it was too risky in such a small community for a new girl suddenly to turn up at school.

There were a lot of factories in Hengelo, and the British started bombing the city in 1943. They didn't want the Germans to be able to use the buildings. So at night we — Aunt Marie, little Wim, and I — often used to huddle together under the stairs. "Don't be frightened," I said to Aunt Marie. "If we die, the three of us will go together." Uncle Kees, who did all kinds of work for the resistance, sometimes used to come and sit with us under the stairs and occasionally there was another person who was in hiding, such as Aunt Marie's youngest brother, Remmert, who'd been ordered to report for the ***Arbeitseinsatz***.[6] Whenever the situation looked dangerous, Uncle Kees would pull up the rug from under the dining table and open the trapdoor, and Remmert would disappear beneath the floor. Then the rug went back and little Wim was placed on top of it, with his building blocks. I remember the Germans coming into the house on two occasions. They were looking for people who had gone into hiding, but all they found were two little blond children playing together.

At the beginning of 1944, the whole family was evacuated to a house on Kwakersplein, a square in Amsterdam. It was just in time — a week after we left, a bomb fell on the house in Hengelo. In Amsterdam I was able to go to school for the first time. I was just part of the family. There were so many newly formed households that no one tried to work out exactly how all of the family members were related. I attended that school for no more than six months at most. I thought it was wonderful. Finally I was among children my own age. But they were so much better than I was at reciting times tables. I'd never done it before.

It was in Amsterdam that I first came to understand what could happen if you were Jewish. That came about because of Danny, one of my classmates, a beautiful boy with dark eyes and black curls. We walked to school together every day until, one morning, I rang his bell and his mother came to the door with puffy red eyes. She told me that Danny was staying with someone and wouldn't be coming to school for a while. Then I suddenly

---

6. ***Arbeitseinsatz***: (German: forced labor) Many German men had been called up to join the army, so Dutch men were taken to Germany to work there toward the end of the war. The men, and sometimes women, were simply rounded up and sent to Germany. Many non-Jewish men tried to escape this forced labor by going into hiding like the Jews.

realized: Was she really his mother? His name isn't Danny Pieterse, I thought, no more than mine is Rita Fonds.

When the **Hunger Winter**[7] began, our school had to close: There was no heating, no food, nothing. I spent all day out on the streets, looking for something to eat. Aunt Marie fixed my long blond hair into two braids so that I would look like a perfect little Nazi girl. Around the corner from where we lived, there was a food depot next to a small ***Wehrmacht***[8] barracks. I used to go there and hang around until a soldier gave me a carrot or a piece of bread.

When I got home, I would proudly say to Aunt Marie, "Look what I've got!"

"How did you get that?" she'd ask.

"Well, I don't say anything to soldiers, but they always come over and start talking to me. 'Hello there, little miss.' Imagine if they knew who I was!"

I used to scour the streets for fuel too. There were small wooden blocks between the tram rails that were perfect for our little camping stoves. It wasn't allowed of course, but everyone used to take the blocks. You had to be careful while you were doing it, though, because if the Germans spotted you, they would drive up and fire their guns. I wasn't strong enough to pull the blocks out by myself, but I was small and thin and fast, and I knew how to put that to good use. I used to sneak up behind people who were whipping out the blocks. I slipped between their legs, swiped a block, threw it into my bag, and got out of there as fast as I could.

---

7. **Hunger Winter** (Dutch: *Hongerwinter*): the Dutch famine in winter 1944–45, when there was a serious shortage of food in much of the Netherlands, causing many people to starve to death.
8. ***Wehrmacht***: the name of the German army from 1935 to 1945.

In the fall of 1944, before that harsh winter really began, we'd gone to stay with some relatives on a farm near Zaandam for a few weeks. We walked ten miles to get there, all the way from Amsterdam. When you're eight years old and you haven't eaten nearly enough, that's a very long way to walk. When we finally arrived, it felt like we were in heaven. They even had real butter on the farm!

But during the Hunger Winter, things became more and more difficult, partly because Aunt Marie was pregnant. She suffered from malnutrition, which caused her legs to swell up so badly that she could hardly stand. So I lined up at the baker's every day, starting at four thirty in the morning, with the hope of getting some bread for my ration coupons. I intended to take care of Aunt Marie, and so I became a little thief who begged for coal at the barracks. At the market, where farmers would still occasionally bring a few carrots, potatoes, and sugar beets to sell, I stole whatever I could lay my hands on.

Since Danny's disappearance, I'd been aware that strange things could happen when you were Jewish, but I still knew nothing about Judaism as a religion. Uncle Kees and Aunt Marie didn't tell me about it, and they raised me as a Protestant. I really enjoyed going to church on Sundays, because the hymns were so lovely. I didn't understand what I was singing, but I thought it sounded absolutely wonderful.

I made friends with a Catholic girl. One day she asked if I'd like to go to church with her sometime. Yes, I said, why not? Well, it was one of those Catholic churches with statues, paintings, rosaries — a big difference from that bare Protestant church. My friend taught me to recite the Hail Mary, in Latin too. I was in seventh heaven. I thought the Catholic religion was so much more beautiful than Protestantism, and they did much more singing too. I asked Uncle Kees and Aunt Marie why we didn't go to a Catholic church. They couldn't give me a convincing answer, but they never tried to force their religion on me either.

Every night, I obediently said my prayers to the Lord Jesus in Heaven, because I thought there was someone up there looking down on me and if I behaved myself he'd think I was a good little girl and do things to help me.

But after liberation, I soon stopped believing. There was a huge party in Amsterdam on May 7, two days after the Netherlands was liberated. Everyone went out onto the streets, including us: Aunt Marie with her big belly, Wim in the baby carriage, and me skipping alongside. We danced and cheered as we headed to Dam Square, right in the center of Amsterdam. But there were still some Germans around, and they opened fire on the crowd from a balcony on a tall building. We hid behind the royal palace as quickly as we could. When we got back home to Kwakersplein at the end of that amazing day, Aunt Marie said, "Well, Rita-pie, you've just got to wait for your parents to get here now. They're sure to come soon, because the war's over and we're all free."

It's not going to happen, I thought. It's not allowed to happen! I never want to leave here! My parents meant nothing to me. There was only one person, or so I believed, who had the power to make sure I could stay with the Fonds family: the good Lord Himself. At night, I got down on my knees and prayed for hours for my parents to let me stay with Aunt Marie and Uncle Kees.

There was one thing I knew for sure: I couldn't abandon Aunt Marie while she was pregnant. I looked after her. She depended on me. But I thought I still had plenty of time. My parents wouldn't come back that soon, would they?

I was wrong about that: In the middle of May, there was a knock at the door. I was playing with my foster brother on the balcony, and I heard Uncle Kees open the door and cry, "Wow, Beb, Frits, fancy you being here so soon!" I immediately knew who they were, and I sat down with my back to the room. Then Aunt Marie called me, "Rita-pie, look who's here!" I heard them coming up the stairs, and I turned around and said, "Hello, ma'am. Hello, sir." That was it. I just went on playing.

Many years later, Uncle Kees told me how he'd pleaded with my father, "Don't take her right now. Leave her here. Just take her out to the zoo for the day first, and then let her stay with you for a night." My father wouldn't hear of it.

Rita, shortly after the war, 1945

I said I wanted to look after Aunt Marie until the baby came. But that didn't persuade my parents. They just took me away. I can't even remember saying good-bye.

And that was the moment I stopped believing. If Our Dear Lord didn't intervene, I was done with him. For two days, I tried saying, "Lord, bless this food, amen," before we ate. And my parents told me, "We don't do that." Fine then, I thought, I don't believe in it anyway.

I heard nothing from Uncle Kees and Aunt Marie. There was no telephone, and it was too far to walk to visit them. I was desperately unhappy. I'd been planning to take care of Aunt Marie until the baby arrived. What was going to happen to her without me? I didn't even hear about the existence of little Inge until two months after the birth. I thought of her as my new baby sister.

I went once with my mother to our old house on Jekerstraat. There was somebody else living there. My mother could see the sunshade that she'd put up herself on the balcony. She wanted to have it for the new house. So we rang the doorbell and asked for it. The house had been cleared out, all except for a painting above the fireplace. "Mom!" I cried. "That's our painting." The people living there didn't even flinch. The house had been assigned to them, along with everything else. We never got the sunshade back.

For a long time, I kept looking for the little boy who had lived next door, but he never came back. And neither did my grandparents or my mother's seven brothers and sisters, the ones my father had arranged hiding places for at the beginning of the war.

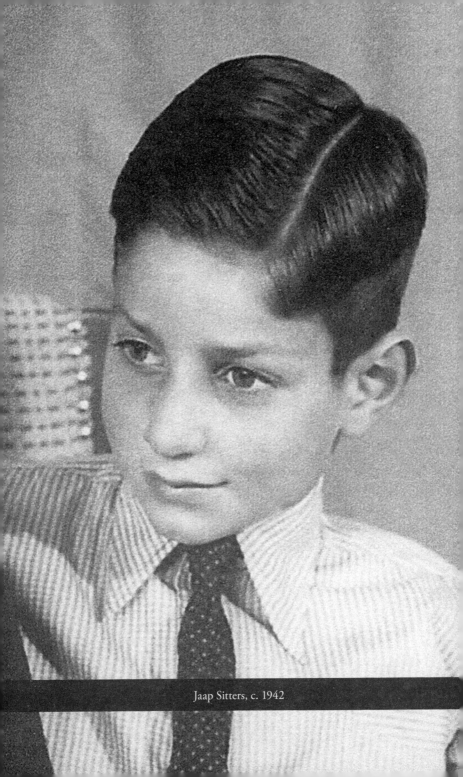

Jaap Sitters, c. 1942

THREE PIANOS

JAAP SITTERS
Born in Naarden, near Amsterdam, on March 29, 1934

Before the war, I was always allowed to go with my father to the local soccer club to watch the matches on Sundays. We sat by the halfway line, me on the grass and him on a green first-aid bag. He was there to help any injured players. "Faster! Faster!" the crowd used to cheer whenever my father ran onto the field.

After the war broke out, he kept that first-aid bag with him at all times. Father was important: He was a member of the Red Cross and he drove around in a new Opel convertible, with a stretcher sticking up from the backseat. Soon after the Netherlands surrendered, Father came home without the car. It had been confiscated by the Germans. He kept the first-aid bag next to his desk, but we never went to watch the soccer matches again.

As I had done before the war, I went on playing with Jopie Hoefnagel,[9] who lived around the corner. He was a couple of years older than me. First we would have a cup of tea with his mother, and then we used to go to our secret hiding place in the garden.

One afternoon we were sitting in our hideaway as usual when he said, "You're going to have to leave school, aren't you? Because you're a Jew." I just stared at him in amazement. I had no idea what he was talking about. I was just about to ask him what he meant when he smacked me really hard, out of the blue. My head was spinning. I had no idea what was going on. Stunned by the shock and the pain, I stood up and walked away. When I got home, I burst into tears. Mother comforted me. She told me that Jopie's parents were **NSB**[10] members and that we were Jewish. I never played with Jopie again after that.

---

9. Pronounced "YOH-pee HOOF-nah-gul."
10. **NSB**: the National Socialist Movement (Dutch: *Nationaal-Socialistische Beweging*), a kind of political party in the Netherlands (1931–45), which was modeled on Adolf Hitler's Nazi Party in Germany. The NSB often worked with the German occupiers.

· · ·

In September 1941, Jopie was proved right. All Jewish children had to go to separate schools. Uncle IJs,[11] a friend of my parents, started a school in a big old house.

The students were a mixed group of all ages. It was fun. But unfortunately, it didn't last for long. Uncle IJs told us that all Jews would soon have to move. "The Germans are going to send out letters with the addresses of where you have to go. And then our little school will have to close."

One morning, our letter arrived. My mother told my sister, Jetty, and me that we all had to move to Amsterdam. We went on the train, each of us carrying a suitcase. That same morning, my father turned the key in the door of our new apartment on Volkerakstraat in Amsterdam. It turned out to be a nice little neighborhood with lots of Jewish children who had also only recently moved in. I had plenty of new friends, and we didn't even have to go to school.

After a few months, another letter came, and we had to move again. Our next apartment was directly opposite the German police garage. Night and day, there were trucks and open-top cars full of yelling Germans driving in and out. I could only sleep with a blanket over my head. At first I didn't know that they were out hunting for Jews. They would bring them back and imprison them in the Hollandsche Schouwburg theater, before sending them to **concentration camps.**[12]

---

11. Pronounced like the English word "ice". IJ is a single letter in Dutch, which is why both letters are capitalized here.
12. **concentration camp:** a large prison camp where people were treated very badly and often died from malnutrition, abuse, or serious illnesses. In many concentration camps, people were murdered, often upon arrival. These camps were known as extermination camps. Two of the best-known camps are Auschwitz-Birkenau and Sobibor. Most of the Dutch Jews were murdered in these two camps.

My father was an optimist. He had a job with the social services department and had managed to get hold of a piece of paper with a special stamp on it, which was called a ***Sperre***.[13] My father said the stamp meant we were not in danger, but when we had to leave again after a few months, even he became less optimistic.

We moved to a district that was occupied solely by Jews. They knew their next address would be **Westerbork**[14] and that would be followed by a "labor camp" in Germany. Stories about what happened to Jews there went buzzing around the neighborhood.

On Friday evenings, my father used to buy something tasty from the Jewish baker's shop and some peanuts in their shells. For a brief moment, the war seemed far away. But later in the evening the mood would change. Then the trucks would come, bringing the German officers shouting their orders. They brought lists of names with them and sent soldiers to the addresses where Jews were to be rounded up. During these raids, people were dragged from their homes and taken away in trucks. Every time they came, we were worried that we might be on the list.

At first, new people moved in soon after families had "left," but later, the houses remained empty. The Germans hammered

---

13. ***Sperre*** (German: block): a stamp in a person's identity card that exempted them from transportation to a concentration camp. The Germans could withdraw the *Sperre* at any moment, which eventually happened in almost every case.

14. **Westerbork**: Before the war, Westerbork was established by the Dutch government as an internment camp for German-Jewish refugees. This changed during the war, when the Germans turned Westerbork into a transit camp. Almost all of the Jews who were rounded up in the Netherlands were sent by train to Westerbork, where they were kept in very primitive conditions. Mainly Jews, but also other groups of "undesirable aliens," were sent first to Westerbork and then on to the concentration and extermination camps. Between July 15, 1942, and September 13, 1944, ninety-three trains headed to the east, carrying 102,000 Jews. Around 5,000 Jews returned to the Netherlands after liberation.

big nails through the doors and into the door frames and then placed a seal on the locks so that they could see no one was living there.

The days crept by until, one day, there was a lot of commotion in the neighborhood. My father announced, "The Germans are coming again tonight and they're taking absolutely everyone this time."

That afternoon, Father went out. When he came back to the apartment, he hammered away at the door for a while. We sat inside, anxiously waiting for him to finish. Finally he came back inside. He told us to sit around the table.

"Okay," he said. "When it gets dark, you all have to be as quiet as mice. We'll close the curtains and turn off the lights. And we'll stop the clock because they might hear the ticking. The door's already locked and I've knocked a nail into the door outside so that it'll look like our apartment's been nailed up, just like the other houses where no one's living. But the door isn't really sealed shut. I sawed the nail in two so it doesn't go all the way through. And I took the seal from an empty house and stuck it over our keyhole to make it look like our apartment's already been emptied. Now we're going to have something to eat. Just some bread, because the smell of cooking might give us away. And then it's time for bed."

Half an hour later, the clock was silent and the house was pitch-dark. I lay in bed, staring at the wall.

I was awakened by the sound of vehicles driving up and stopping nearby. Orders shouted in German, stamping of boots, people wailing. I sneaked out of bed and felt my way in the darkness to the living room. Father and Mother were already there,

**Zentralstelle für jüdische
Auswanderung Amsterdam**
Adama v. Scheltemaplein 1
Telefoon 97001

N⁰ 134816

OPROEPING!

Aan   Sitters, Jacob Emanuel   L   **No.**
29.3.34   Hertzogstraat 6 III

U moet zich voor eventueele deelname aan een, onder politietoezichtstaande, werk-verruiming in Duitschland voor persoonsonderzoek en geneeskundige keuring naar het door-gangskamp Westerbork, station Hooghalen, begeven.

Daartoe moet U op .... om .... uur

op de verzamelplaats .... aanwezig zijn

Als bagage mag medegenomen worden:

        1   **koffer of rugzak**
        1   **paar werklaarzen**
        2   **paar sokken**
        2   **onderbroeken**
        2   **hemden**
        1   **werkpak**
        2   **wollen dekens**
        2   stel beddengoed (overtrek met laken)
        1   **eetnap**
        1   **drinkbeker**
        1   **lepel en**
        1   **pullover**
             handdoek en toiletartikelen

en eveneens marschproviand voor 3 dagen en alle aan U uitgereikte distributiekaarten met inbegrip van de distributiestamkaart.

De mee te nemen bagage moet in gedeelten gepakt worden.

a.   Noodzakelijke reisbehoeften
        daartoe behooren: 2 dekens, 1 stel beddegoed, levensmiddelen voor 3 dagen, toiletgerei, etensbord, eetbestek, drinkbeker,

b.   Groote bagage
        De onder b. vermelde bagage moet worden gepakt in een stevige koffer of rugzak, welke op duidelijke wijze voorzien moet zijn van **naam, voornamen, geboortedatum en het woord „Holland".**
        Gezinsbagage is niet toegestaan.
        Het voorgaande moet nauwkeurig in acht genomen worden, daar de groote bagage in de plaats van vertrek afzonderlijk ingeladen wordt.
        De verschillende bewijs- en persoonspapieren en distributiekaarten met inbegrip van de distributiestamkaart mogen **niet bij de bagage verpakt worden,** doch moeten, voor onmiddellijk vertoon gereed, medegedragen worden.
        De woning moet ordelijk achtergelaten en afgesloten worden, de huissleutels moeten worden medegenomen.
        Niet medegenomen mogen worden: levend huisraad.

K 372

Jaap's letter of deportation to Westerbork, which includes a list of items to be brought to the camp: a pair of work boots, a set of work clothes, two blankets, bedclothes, a towel, toiletries, two pairs of socks, two sets of underwear, a sweater, a bowl, a spoon, a cup, and enough food for three days. People were told to leave their houses locked up and were not allowed to bring pets.

and Jetty wasn't far behind me. We heard the Germans breaking through the door downstairs. There was an elderly couple living on the floor above us. I didn't know them, but I heard them wailing that night as the Germans beat them down the stairs.

Then the Germans came back up. We could hear their voices outside our door. It seemed to go on forever. Finally the footsteps went away. Then we heard the engine start up, and they drove on and stopped outside the next house.

When I came into the living room the next morning, Father and Mother were already dressed. The curtains were closed and there was a strange atmosphere in the house. It was so quiet. Everything was silent. The table was laid differently. No tablecloth, just a package. "That's some food for the journey," said Mother. "Your father will explain the rest."

"There's absolutely no one else living in the entire neighborhood now," he said. "The stores are all closed and it's too dangerous to buy food outside the area. We have to leave. And it's too risky for all of us to go together. Our only option is to leave one by one."

Jetty and I weren't told where Father and Mother were going, and I wasn't allowed to hear Jetty's new address either. It was my turn first, and Jetty was sent to her room.

So there we were, just the three of us. Father said, "Do you remember how to get to Aunt Toni and Uncle Jo's place?"

I shook my head.

"I'll explain it to you. It's easy. You go around the corner here and then turn right by the stores and walk all the way down Middenweg." He pointed at my right arm, just to make certain. "After Middenweg, you just keep on going," Father continued. "Straight on, for about five hours. If you do that, you'll eventually see that street where you always used to meet me when I came home from work. You know the way from there."

Then he gave me a stern look. "And remember, it'll take you a long time to get there, a really, really long time, and you can't leave until dusk, when it'll be quieter and safer. If you hear a car coming, get off the road until it's gone past."

Mother removed all of the stars from our clothes that day. At sundown, we said a quick good-bye, and off I went. Getting to Middenweg wasn't a problem. Turn right and keep going straight on. I walked along briskly.

After about half an hour, I wasn't quite so sure. Was I going the right way? I seemed to have been walking forever. The bag of food and drink was getting heavier with every step. At one point I stopped to eat something. I think I fell asleep for a while too.

It was pitch-dark by then. I tried to keep my spirits up by talking to myself out loud. I finally arrived in Bussum, the town where Aunt Toni and Uncle Jo lived. I have no idea how I did it, but I know that I've never been so tired in my life.

Aunt Toni and Uncle Jo lived in a big, grand house. They were just as I remembered: Aunt Toni was kind, and Uncle Jo was bald. He smoked cigars and wore glasses with thick dark frames. They rented out rooms, and I was introduced to some of the residents as soon as I got there. There was Aunt Job, a kind, gray-haired lady, and Aunt Moeke,[15] who wasn't as gray but was also nice. And there was a scary man with a red beard.

15. Pronounced "MOO-kuh."

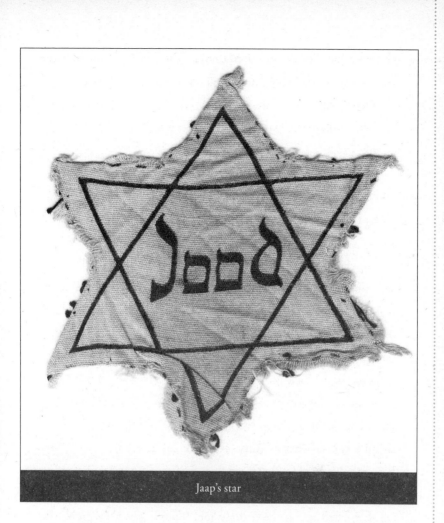

Jaap's star

Then Aunt Toni took me up to the attic, where I would sleep. "If you can't get to sleep, just come downstairs," she said.

When she woke me the next morning, I saw that I'd been sleeping in a nice, cozy room with a sloping ceiling.

"This used to be a guest room," Aunt Toni told me. "But now it's yours."

There was a curtained partition in the room with space behind it for clothes. She opened the curtain and pushed the clothes aside. "You might need to hide from the Germans at some point." At the back of the space, almost invisible, there was a wooden panel.

She pulled the panel away. "Here's a flashlight. Go take a look."

There was a mattress on the floor, with some blankets on it, and a chamber pot with a blue rim. "You mustn't tell anyone about this. And you're only allowed in there when Uncle Jo and I say so."

Uncle Jo, who worked for the newspaper, left early every morning. When he went out, he tucked his slim briefcase under his arm so that no one could see the yellow star. He and Aunt Toni had a mixed marriage, which meant that Uncle Jo hadn't been forced to move to Amsterdam.

One day, Uncle Jo called up to me. "Surprise!" he said. He took me to the garage, where Aunt Toni was standing beside a magnificent rabbit hutch with two tiny little rabbits in it. "You're to take care of them," Aunt Toni said in a serious voice. "You have to give them food and water and freshen up the straw once a week. And you have to clean out the cage every day."

It turned out to be a dirty job. The bigger they grew, the larger the droppings were. Then one of the rabbits started to pull out the fur on its chest — in great big clumps! "That's what female rabbits do when they become adults," Uncle Jo reassured me. "It means they want to build a nest."

Soon there were five little creatures in the nest. Those ugly little things soon turned into cute little mini-rabbits. We needed three more hutches, and I was very busy.

I had one rabbit that was my favorite: Sijbeltje.[16] Her mother had rejected her. Uncle Jo made a hole in a cork and poked a thin tube through it to make a feeding bottle. Sijbeltje grew well, just like her brothers and sisters. More nests were built. More hutches were added. Before I knew it, I had twenty-three big adult rabbits in ten hutches! And Sijbeltje, of course. She was *my* rabbit. I loved her and she loved me.

"All of those rabbits are a lot of work," said Uncle Jo one day. "And we can't build any more hutches in the garage. It's difficult to get hold of enough food for them too. We're going to have to get rid of them."

I nodded. "But I want to keep Sijbeltje."

Uncle Jo said I could.

A day or two later, when I wasn't allowed into the garage, I thought someone must have come for the rabbits. It wasn't until later that I realized the whole house smelled of cooked meat. I rushed downstairs. Aunt Toni and Uncle Jo and a really big man were at work in the kitchen. The counter was covered with skinned rabbits, and there were pans on the boil. I started crying and screaming, "Where's Sijbeltje? Where's Sijbeltje?"

They told me that she was safe and sound in her hutch.

I ran to the garage. There, in the corner, was our original hutch, with one large, reddish-brown rabbit inside. But it wasn't my Sijbeltje!

We ate rabbit once a week after that. Everyone thought it was delicious and they all praised me for taking such good care of

---

16. Pronounced "SAY-bul-chuh."

them. But I was never able to eat a single bite. Just the thought that one of those rabbits was my Sijbeltje made me feel sick.

Uncle Jo had started to work less and was doing more painting instead. He had an easel, a palette, brushes, and a big box with tubes of paint in every color. The back room was his workroom, where he painted his still lifes, like bowls of apples and pears, or a cigarette in an ashtray. One time he painted a bunch of grapes with a few drops of water on them. It was really good.

He hung all of his paintings in ornate gold frames. I spent so many hours with Uncle Jo that Aunt Toni thought it would be a good idea for him to teach me to paint. "He'll have to learn how to draw first," said Uncle Jo.

From then on, Uncle Jo and I did art together. I enjoyed it more and more. Uncle Jo thought it was time for me to start signing my drawings. "What do you mean?" I asked.

"You have to put your signature on your work. Your artistic pseudonym." Then he explained to me what a pseudonym was — and I started racking my brain to come up with a good name. Everyone in the house became involved, and we finally settled on Jelle Stout. Jelle, because it was a name from Friesland, in the north of the Netherlands. "There are no Jews in Friesland," they said. So that was perfect. And everyone liked Stout because it means naughty in Dutch, but also bold and wild.

So I signed my scrawls as Jelle Stout.

Uncle Sjaak,[17] Uncle Jo's brother, often used to visit. He was also married to a woman of German descent, Aunt Annie.

---

17. Pronounced "SHAAK."

Sometimes they brought their only son, Hans, with them. I didn't like Hans at all.

Uncle Sjaak always had a violin with him. When he was out on the street, he used to hold his violin case in front of his yellow star, just as Uncle Jo did with his briefcase. At home, they'd have tea and then Uncle Sjaak would take out his violin. As soon as she heard Uncle Sjaak start to play, Aunt Moeke came downstairs. She would sit down at the piano and dramatically hit four notes, and then Uncle Sjaak would take his time tuning his violin. After a while, he started scraping away, and the performance wasn't improved when Aunt Moeke sang along in her high, quavering voice. I used to sneak out of the room as soon as Aunt Toni had passed around the homemade apple pie.

"You'll have to go into the hiding place tonight," said Aunt Toni one day. Uncle Sjaak had been picked up by the Germans. His son, Hans, was going to sleep in my room that night, and he wasn't allowed to know that I was living there, so I had to be hidden by the time he came home from school. I crawled into the hiding place with a flashlight and a blanket just after four, made up my bed, and turned off the flashlight. I tried to think of nice things. After a while, I really needed to go to the bathroom. So I turned on the flashlight, and I went in search of the chamber pot with the blue rim.

I was awakened by stomping on the stairs. "Ugh!" said Hans, as he came into the room. "It stinks in here!" I could hear him taking off his clothes, and before long the springs were squeaking as he lay down in my bed. I didn't dare to turn over onto my other side.

I had to sleep in the hiding place more and more often because there had been a warning about house searches. Luckily it always turned out to be a false alarm, but the tension really affected the atmosphere in the house.

One night I went to say good night to Uncle Jo, just as he was about to start his daily game of chess with the scary man with the red beard. "Let's play for the little Jew boy tonight," said the scary man. I knew right away that he was talking about me. I told Aunt Toni what I'd heard. She tried to reassure me.

The next morning, some Germans appeared on the gravel path. Aunt Toni hissed, "Scram! Upstairs!"

I flew upstairs and into my hiding place. A while later, Aunt Toni came to fetch me. "They were here for Uncle Jo, but he was at work."

They picked up Uncle Jo at the newspaper and held him for a couple of weeks. I couldn't stay in Bussum any longer. Aunt Toni and Uncle Jo had some acquaintances who knew someone in the resistance, and they were able to track down my parents' address. Eventually it was decided that they would find a place for me with them, so the man from the resistance took me to my parents, whom I hadn't seen for more than a year. Father hugged me tight, and Mother didn't seem to ever want to let me go. She just kept kissing me and quietly singing the songs she had sung before the war.

The same man from the resistance moved us to another house. We lived there with a young woman, and my parents didn't like her at all. I thought she was nice, though. She was always cheerful, which is more than could be said of my mother and father. Sometimes I was awakened at nights by giggling and deep male voices speaking German.

One morning, Father started sawing a hatch in the cupboard beneath the stairs. There was a space of around thirty inches beneath the floor that might work as a place to hide. There was just enough room to lie down in the sand, but you couldn't even crouch in there. My father asked me to climb in to see what it was like, and then he closed the hatch. I was terrified.

The village of Hoograven was so deserted in the daytime that Father thought it was safe enough to go out for a walk. It was wonderful: sunlight, fresh air. On one of our outings, we found a nice little canal. "Hey," he said, "I have a couple of fishing rods in the shed. Why don't we try them out?"

So a couple of days later, we headed out, both carrying a fishing rod. As we were approaching the canal, Father suddenly said, "Keep walking, just keep on walking!"

He had seen two soldiers with rifles walking toward us.

A few seconds later, we came face-to-face with them. I had never been so close to "the enemy" before. First I saw their boots. I had to look up to see their faces. Big helmets, big dark sunglasses, and very big guns.

"Off fishing, are you?" one of them said, looking at me.

They had what was almost a friendly conversation with my father. In Dutch, not German! After a few minutes, they allowed us to go on our way.

"Good fishing!" one of them said. The other patted me on the head.

We walked on in silence. As soon as we were out of sight, my father hissed, "Back home! I know one of them, and he recognized me too."

We took a detour home, walking faster and faster as we went. Father kept looking over his shoulder. I'd never seen him so anxious before.

When I was getting ready for bed, he said, "You'd better sleep in the hiding place this evening."

The thought of it made me shiver, but I didn't dare admit that. I slid into the hiding place an hour later, carrying a woolen blanket. Feet first, then the rest of me. It wasn't easy.

Finally I was in position. The hatch went down. The wooden floor was directly above my nose. I lay there on the sand, wrapped up in my blanket. It was pitch-dark. For a while I could still hear muffled voices. Then nothing.

I woke up some time in the night. It was cold. As soon as I remembered where I was, I started to panic. The sand was so wet. I heard someone screaming, and I realized it was me. I flew out of the hiding place. There was no one in the living room. I tiptoed back to my own bed, where I shivered with cold as I waited for the night to end.

I was still shaking when I went downstairs the next morning. The woman who was sheltering us gave me a cup of tea. And after a while, Mother and Father came out from their hiding place. They were shaking all over as well. "Come along," said Mother, pushing me up the stairs. "Let's get you into some dry clothes."

She told me that the Germans had broken through the dikes to put a stop to the **Allied**[18] advance. As a result, large areas of land were now underwater, and the level of the groundwater in

---

18. **Allies**: the countries that fought together against the Germans in World War II, which included Canada, France, Poland, the Soviet Union, the United Kingdom, and the United States.

the local villages had risen. That's why the sand down in the hole had been so wet!

Late that evening, the man from the resistance took us to a new address.

Together with a number of other Jewish people, we were now hiding in a big old house on Stadhouderslaan, an elegant avenue on the outskirts of Utrecht. The couple who owned the house made good money from the people who were in hiding there. She was really bossy and not eager to help. He used to cook and clean, and he sang all day long in a strange high-pitched girlish voice.

Downstairs was a cluttered basement that ran the length of the whole house. Hardly anyone ever went down there. The back door led to a large yard with a high fence all around. After that, the meadows began. It was a great place. Finally I had somewhere I could play soccer.

One day we heard someone banging on the front door. "Upstairs!" called Father.

We flew to our hiding place between the first and second stories. Both floors, upstairs and downstairs, were made up of rooms that were separated by sliding doors and closets. You got to the hiding place by lifting up the floor of the closet in the room upstairs, and then slipping into the space above the closet downstairs. Three or four people could squeeze into the gap above each of the closets. There was barely enough room for one person in the space above the sliding doors, but that was my hiding place.

I heard the sound of army boots in the corridor and the Germans growing closer and closer. I was terrified. They were sure to hear my heart pounding and the others breathing. They banged on the walls, looking for hollow spaces. Finally the noises died down, and the front door opened and closed. We'd been lucky. But we didn't know if someone had betrayed us.

Not long after that, the Germans came back, in the middle of the day. I was playing in the basement and hadn't heard the banging on the door. A few of the others ran past me on their way outside to hide in the drainage ditch around the meadow. You got there through a hole in the fence.

Before I knew it, I was alone again. Then I heard Father at the top of the stairs, "Jaap, find somewhere to hide! We'll be in the hiding place upstairs."

There was no time to reply. The basement door was opening again. I had to do something. I was standing next to the metal trash can, so I took off the lid, jumped inside, and pulled the lid back down over my head. Footsteps came closer and then stopped at the trash can. Someone lifted the lid.

There was no order yelled in German. No one dragged me out of the trash can. Instead, someone dumped a load of vegetable peelings and other trash on my head and replaced the lid. I didn't move until the basement door opened again and my father called down, "You can come out now. It's safe!"

I lifted the lid and crawled out from among the peelings. My father couldn't stop laughing. He told me to stay there while he fetched my mother. She comforted me and cleaned my face. The cloth she used turned red from all the beet peelings.

That night, our man from the resistance paid us an unexpected visit. He had a big bag with him. He'd been to see a local farmer and had exchanged sheets and blankets for food. He opened the bag and took out an enormous ham and bread and what must have been a hundred eggs. It felt like a party! The whole place soon smelled wonderful, as the fried eggs sputtered away on our camping stove. I could hardly wait. Such a feast! I wolfed it down, but the whole lot soon came back up again because my stomach could no longer cope with the fat.

In the days that followed, I was often hungry, and I had problems with a boil on my arm. The man from the resistance stopped coming to visit. For me, that was the worst period of the war. Our firewood supply was getting low, so we chopped up anything that would burn and made it into little sticks. We set fire to the stair rail and the garden fence had to go — all that was left was a small section beside the house that would shield us if we needed to escape into the meadow. But we had heard that the liberators were coming closer.

One evening there was another bang on the door. We all dashed to our hiding places, and I was soon inside my little space above the sliding doors. There were three more people hiding on top of the closet, close to my head.

The Germans made lots of noise as they came upstairs, and they stabbed their bayonets into the wall. Then what we'd always feared actually happened: A bayonet went through the thin wallpaper above the closet, exposing the three people who were hiding there. *"Raus!"* cried the Germans. "Out!"

One by one, they scrambled down. The Germans didn't see me lying there in the small space. After what seemed like an eternity, I dared to peep out. The room was empty.

Father and Mother had hidden with two other people out in

the meadow. They came back after a while. Everyone was very shaken, but they kept saying how brave I'd been.

During the last weeks of the war, all we talked about was liberation. Father had torn a map of Europe out of an atlas, and he stuck a pin in the map in all the places where the Germans were retreating. He tied a red thread from pin to pin so that we could see exactly how far away the liberators were. The red thread was moving closer and closer to our house.

One fine morning, the big day came. "Go outside," said Father.

Outside? "Is the war over?" I asked.

It was absolutely silent on our street. Feeling rather uneasy, I walked over to Biltstraat, where I saw a whole crowd of people. Right by our street there were German army trucks full of soldiers. They waved at me as I walked past. One of them signaled at me to wait and then slipped me a currant bun. I hesitated: Could I accept something from a German? But I was so hungry that I ate it all up. It was delicious.

I walked on to find thousands of people lining the street and Dutch flags everywhere I looked. I squeezed my way to the front. Then a wave of excitement passed through the crowd: A green jeep was approaching in the distance. There were two soldiers in it and a crowd of people swarming around them. They were kissing and hugging the soldiers, and everyone wanted to touch them. The jeep had to pull over.

Then we heard a deep rumbling: It was a tank with a big gun. The crowd stepped back and the jeep started moving again. They were all jumping up onto the tank. People sat on the barrel of the gun and rode along on the tank. Lots of other army vehicles drove along behind.

I wanted to join in the procession, but I couldn't see any space for me. But then a small truck with a trailer came by. Before I knew what I was doing, I was already sitting up on the bar between the truck and the trailer. I rode along slowly, waving at the crowd lining the street. It was wonderful.

Then I started to find it tricky to keep my balance, and I had to concentrate on holding on instead of waving. I wanted to get down, so I decided to jump as we went around a curve, but my pants were caught. I screamed and screamed. My screams were even louder than the rest of the noise. The procession came to a stop, and someone freed me.

The authorities gave us a place to live in Bussum, but that house needed a lot of repairs, so we all went to stay with Aunt Toni. My sister had also gotten through the war in hiding. But Uncle Jo didn't survive: He died of a heart attack the day before liberation.

It wasn't that easy to get back all of the things that we'd left with friends and acquaintances. No one had expected that the Sitters family would still be alive.

We'd been back in Bussum a few weeks when our black piano was returned. Less than a week after that, we got the small piano that had belonged to Uncle Dee and Aunt Floor. I hardly ever played it.

A third piano came some weeks later, together with some other things that had belonged to our aunts and uncles. Gradually it became clear that, out of all our relatives, ours was the only family to have survived.

Bloeme Emden, December 17, 1941

I'LL GO FETCH
HER TOMORROW

BLOEME EMDEN
Born in Amsterdam, July 5, 1926

After liberation, on my way back to the Netherlands, I sent a postcard to the house on Rijnstraat in Amsterdam that had been my safe house during the war. I wrote to say that I'd survived Auschwitz and was coming home. I got there a few weeks later. It was evening and Rijnstraat was bare, as all of the trees had been chopped down for firewood. As I climbed the steps of the Van Moppes family's house, I wondered what to expect. Freddy, my boyfriend, opened the door. I was bald and emaciated. He didn't recognize me until I spoke. Everything about you can change, but voices stay the same. He hugged me and called to his parents, "Come see who's here!" They welcomed me warmly, very warmly indeed. They'd been expecting me ever since they'd received my postcard. Freddy's father was based at Amsterdam's central train station as a Red Cross worker, and he'd scoured the platforms for me every day. His mother had sat waiting at the window. "I have two dresses," she said. "One of them's for you."

Around four years earlier, as I was cycling near Rijnstraat, I suddenly realized just how serious the situation was. Hitler's words came booming out of large loudspeakers, which hung in the trees every couple of hundred yards: *"Wir werden die Juden ausrotten, ausrotten, ausrotten."* (We will eradicate the Jews! Eradicate them! Eradicate them!) I made a decision: I am not going to allow myself to be eradicated. But I was also aware that it would be very hard to hide away from all that violence.

Until then I had been patient and let the war happen around me. I used to think: We're not allowed to walk down the street anymore? Fine, then we won't go for a walk. Then we won't go to the theater. Then we won't go to the library. Or out shopping. I saw all of their rules as harassment that we could live with. I only really became frightened when the deportations started and Jews were taken away and families torn apart. The first call-ups started arriving in early July 1942, which is when we received ours. The orders were cunningly vague, stating the date and the place you were to report to, and that you should take clothing, a mug, and cutlery. I had turned sixteen at the beginning of July, and like many of my classmates, I was part of the first group to be called up: Jews between the ages of sixteen and thirty-five. Most people obeyed the order. "We're young and strong," they said. "We know we'll have to work hard but there's no way out, because we're registered and they know who we are."

My father was so desperate that he went to visit the office that was responsible for the deportations. He said to the first German he saw, "My daughter can't go." The man looked at him in surprise, but he took the call-up papers and put a stamp on them to say that I was exempted from deportation "until further notice." This temporary exemption was called a *Sperre*. When the deportations first started, it was still possible to win over some of the Germans. That all changed later on. My parents also had a *Sperre*, so they would not be deported for the time being either. My father had once been a diamond cutter, and although he had had a different job for years, the Germans thought that people who knew about diamonds might be useful in the future.

So I went back to school. It was a school that was just for Jewish children. Our classroom grew emptier and emptier as my fellow students were deported or went into hiding. At the beginning of May 1943, I did my final written examinations, with two other classmates. By the time of the oral exam, a few weeks later,

I was the only one left, but the twelve exams, spread over two days, went ahead as usual.

At the end of the first morning, after the first four exams, Freddy was waiting for me at the school door. My mother had received a visit from some "gentlemen" who had come to fetch me. Apparently my *Sperre* had been withdrawn. So "until further notice" meant until today. They were going to come back for me at eight o'clock. They said that if I wasn't there, they would take my parents and my sister.

As we were talking, the air-raid siren went off. Everyone hurried inside. We went into the school. I had a flash of inspiration, and I went to the school principal. I explained what had happened and asked if he could arrange for me to take the remaining eight examinations that afternoon. The principal managed to get everyone together. I was the very last student in the school and the only student in two classes to take the complete set of leaving examinations. There was a brief meeting and then they called me in and gave me my diploma.

That afternoon I didn't think seriously about going into hiding. It was a horrible thought that the "gentlemen" might take my parents and my sister instead. Besides that, going into hiding was not something you could do at the drop of a hat. My mother had wanted to go into hiding, but my father was too scared, because if you got caught, you were automatically deported as a criminal. The Germans did everything they could to make people believe there was nothing to be scared of if you followed the rules. But if you broke them, then things could go very badly. We never thought their ultimate intention was to murder everyone though. That was too awful to imagine.

When I came out with my diploma, Freddy was waiting out-side again. He took me to his parents' house, where we ate dinner. I got home a little before eight. At five past eight, the "gentlemen" came. My parents were distraught when we said good-bye. My sister, Via, cried and waved after me through the window. Carrying my shoulder bag and a backpack, I followed the men to the police station, where I found other Jews waiting. We spent the night there, slumped on the floor and trying to sleep.

Shortly before I left, my mother suggested that I should try to join up with a family, as they might be able to protect me and give me advice. I soon met a suitable family at the police station. They had some younger children and agreed to "adopt" me as their eldest daughter.

The next morning, the Germans took us to the **Hollandsche Schouwburg**.[19] It was a famous theater in Amsterdam and until recently had been one of the few places where Jews were still allowed to perform and to attend shows. Now it was an assembly point where Jews from Amsterdam and the surrounding area were held while awaiting deportation. As people entered, their names and addresses were noted so that the Germans knew exactly which Jews they had in the theater. This also allowed them to make up lists of names and dates for transportations. They called it registration. I didn't want to be registered. If they didn't know I was inside, they wouldn't miss me if I managed to escape. As everyone lined up, I pushed my backpack forward a

---

19. **Hollandsche Schouwburg**: a theater in Amsterdam that the German occupiers used between August 1942 and November 1943 to imprison Jews before they were sent to con-centration camps. Young children of families held there were taken to a kindergarten across the street.

couple of feet, then I walked back to fetch my shoulder bag and put it down a little in front of the backpack. I shuffled around and tried to make myself look busy, and that's how I got inside the Schouwburg without being registered.

The atmosphere in the building was awful. Everyone was anxiously wondering what was going to happen to them. I felt so lonely without my family, without my boyfriend. There were hardly any bathrooms in the building, and you had to wait endlessly in line for food.

When I was in the Schouwburg, I received a nice letter from my parents, with a number written in the margin: 339. It was the number of a house on Orteliusstraat, where Truus and her husband, Floor, lived, acquaintances of my father's who had offered several times to organize a place for us to hide.

Hollandsche Schouwburg, Amsterdam, the Netherlands

I knew that one of my cousin's friends worked at the Schouwburg. Everyone called him Bul. It was days before I saw him. When I did, I stopped him and said, "I want to get out of here."

"You and everyone else," he replied.

"But I'm not registered."

"Ah, that changes things." He said he'd see what he could do for me.

A few days later, Bul came up to me and said, "You're leaving tomorrow. At four in the afternoon, they'll ring the bell to tell the children up to the age of fourteen to gather in the lobby to be escorted across the street to the kindergarten. You can go with them. Just pretend you're one of the supervisors. Stay in the kindergarten for the night, and get out of there the next day."

I was so nervous the following day that I got clumsy and split the seam at the back of my shoe. There was a cobbler in the Schouwburg who offered to repair the shoe for me. I gave it to him and he said he'd bring it back in a couple of hours. But he didn't. And it was almost four. So I came up with the idea of asking my new "family" to send the shoe to the kindergarten. I told them what I was planning, but they strongly advised me not to try to escape: It was far too dangerous. When I told them that my mind was made up, they promised they'd do their best to help.

The bell sounded and I hurried to the lobby. I was the first one there, because the children naturally wanted to stay with their parents for as long as possible. There I stood, with one shoe and one sock. Suddenly the guard at the door turned around and shouted, *"Was machen Sie da?"* What are you up to?

I froze. I couldn't say a word or move a muscle. The man looked at me, and his gaze moved down to my shoeless foot. Then he shrugged his shoulders and turned back to look at the street. The children came and we crossed the street to the kindergarten, where I was to spend the night. It was far too risky to run away immediately. The Germans kept a really close eye on us. A few hours later, to my astonishment, a courier finally delivered my shoe to me at the kindergarten.

Early the next morning, I went out on the street. The people at the kindergarten had explained to me that you couldn't just slip away. If you wanted to keep out of sight of the Germans across the street, you had to wait for the tram to pull up at the stop in front of the kindergarten. When the tram moved off, you walked along with it and quickly took the first right-hand turn. It worked. There I was, walking along the street, anxiously holding my purse in front of my star. It was a beautiful May morning, and the day

A tram running in front of the Hollandsche Schouwburg, carrying Jews guarded by soldiers

soon became warmer. I was wearing a thick winter coat, which my mother had told me to take.

But, on my way to Orteliusstraat, I got lost. When I arrived there a few hours later, there was no one home. I walked around the block and rang again. Still no one. I knew it was a really dangerous situation. If I was stopped, they'd send me straight back to the Schouwburg. Then I remembered that I had relatives with a butcher's shop on Kinkerstraat, not far from Orteliusstraat. As far as I knew, Uncle Karel and Aunt Martha hadn't been deported yet. They were exempt from deportation because they ran a *Joods Lokaal*, a store for Jews run by Jews.

The shop was open. My aunt and uncle thought I was a ghost when I walked in, because they knew I'd been taken away. Somehow, they managed to reach my parents. They came over and we spent some time together that afternoon on the floor above the butcher's shop. It was the last time I saw them.

When I went to Orteliusstraat again at six that evening, Truus and Floor had returned from work. They were pleased to see me, and I felt very welcome. Floor went to my parents' house a few times to fetch things, and my mother and father used the last of their money to buy a fake identity card for me. People from the resistance had inserted my photograph and a thumbprint onto the card, so now my name was Nancy Winifred Altman, born in Indonesia on August 22, 1924, and currently residing in Epe.

Floor and Truus lived in a three-room apartment. I was given one of the rooms to myself, which was a real luxury. Of course I had to keep to the rules of hiding: Only flush the toilet when someone was at home, go straight to my room when there were visitors, and never answer the door. Truus and Floor worked for the resistance and were involved in distributing illegal newspapers. One evening they were expecting a large delivery. Truus had gone out for a while and the doorbell rang, and then again a little later, and again, so I was almost certain it was the man with the newspapers and of course I knew someone had to accept the delivery. But I wasn't allowed to open the door, ever. Whatever I decided to do, there was going to be trouble. I didn't go to the door, and that meant a resistance man had had to wander the streets with his dangerous delivery.

With all the illegal work that Truus and Floor were doing, it became too risky for me to stay at Orteliusstraat. "If we get caught, they'll get you too." So they looked for a new address for me. What followed for me was a list of over fifteen addresses. Every time I moved, I wondered how I should behave, what the family thought was polite, and what would annoy them.

I was very lucky to have a fall-back address: my boyfriend Freddy's house on Rijnstraat. In an absolute emergency, I could go there. Freddy had a Jewish father and a non-Jewish mother, so the family was exempt from deportation for the time being. Although Freddy's mother was clearly nervous about it, they always made me feel welcome, and I could stay there for a few days. I used to have Freddy's room, and he would sleep in the drawing room.

One morning when I was there, I was awakened by strange noises. Going to investigate seemed like a bad idea. Freddy's father was a diamond cutter. The Germans suspected him of having diamonds in the house, which should have been handed over long ago. They searched the place very thoroughly, but somehow they forgot the room where I was anxiously waiting for them to finish.

It was such an incredible stroke of luck. Why didn't they come into my room? It was a series of lucky incidents like that that allowed me to survive the war.

I was able to seek refuge on Hobbemakade, in a house that had been abandoned but was still fully furnished. The Jews who had lived there had already been taken away. Someone from the resistance brought me food every day and stopped for a quick chat, but it was such a lonely place. I felt sad and abandoned.

I didn't stay at that address for long either. We knew that the house might be emptied at any moment. They called it "Pulsing," after Abraham Puls, the owner of the removal company that came to take everything away. And that's how I ended up staying with Tine and Herman Waage-Kramer, who were also in the resistance. They had other Jews hiding in their four-room apartment on Bronckhorststraat, including an invalid. There was always enough room for emergency cases too.

One day Tine said she thought she'd found a job for me in the town of Amersfoort, about thirty miles from Amsterdam. I was going to work as a maid for two elderly ladies. Tine took me to their house and told me to wait in a separate room while she talked to them. Tine came back a little later, "We're going back to Amsterdam, Nancy." When we got outside, she told me that the women didn't want me because I looked too Jewish. Soon after that we heard that there was going to be a raid at the house on Bronckhorststraat. We packed up the entire house in half a day and fled to an empty house on Merwedeplein. And sure enough, there was a raid that night.

During that period, Steven, one of the resistance workers, had spent hours talking to my parents, trying to persuade them to send my little sister, Via, into hiding. Finally they agreed, partly because they'd been promised that Via would be with me at first. Steven was going to pick her up on the evening of June 19, 1943. He got home late, without my sister. He'd had a bad day, and he was exhausted. "Tomorrow morning," he said. "I'll go fetch her tomorrow."

The next morning, on June 20, 1943, there was a major round-up in south Amsterdam, and all of the remaining Jews were dragged from their homes. My parents and my sister were picked up and sent directly to Sobibor. Even now, I still find that so hard to live with: just one day too late. Some weeks later, Tine did not come home one evening. We waited and waited. A few anxious hours passed, and then we heard that the resistance group she belonged to had been rounded up. Everyone left the house. Only Steven and I stayed behind. We spent the night in a hiding place in the bathroom. The next morning I went back to my emergency address, with Freddy's parents on Rijnstraat.

There were staff shortages because of the war, so I found a job as an assistant in a home for well-to-do elderly people without anyone asking too many questions. I was in hiding there for nine months and during that time I must have mopped hundreds of miles of corridors. But I thought it was wonderful. I was happy to be able to do something useful. I used to take meals to the old people as well, and coffee and tea and glasses of water. On Sunday evenings, we sang hymns together in the main room.

I slept in the attic, in a room with three other girls. We each had a bed and our own nightstand. Ida, one of my roommates, often used to say, "You're a Jewess, and I'm going to report you." I had no idea how I was supposed to react. Whenever she made her threats, I used to break out in a cold sweat. But she never gave me away.

The superintendent was a small woman who wore a brown nurse's uniform with a matching cap. She was very strict, and she treated me unkindly. Whenever something was stolen from the old people, which happened frequently, I was the prime suspect. She always made me hand over the key to my nightstand, which I found very insulting.

Early one morning, the superintendent called me into her office. The Germans had taken a number of Jewish patients from their beds that night. She said I had to disappear because they were going to come back. Once again I had to make use of my emergency address with the Van Moppes family.

In May 1944, the resistance organizations in Amsterdam made contact with their counterparts in Rotterdam: Aad Zegers and his sister, Mary ten Have-Zegers. One of the women in Mary's swimming club needed a maid. Mary had said she knew someone in Amsterdam, a decent girl. Mary told me not to say that I was Jewish and in hiding, so we decided to tell her that I was engaged and had decided to work for a year as a maid in order to pick up the finer points of housekeeping.

Mrs. Lindijer took me on straightaway. She was a widow, and she shared the house with her son, a minister. I was given my own room. I got along well with the lady of the house. She soon started to take me out shopping with her, which I didn't really like, because it was too dangerous, but it still felt wonderful to be outside for a while. Freddy came to Rotterdam a few times as well, so I was able to introduce my fiancé to them.

After two pleasant months, Mrs. Lindijer said to me one morning, "Nancy, we're going on vacation for two weeks and you can have the time off too." I acted as though I was delighted, but in reality I was terrified. Where could I go? As soon as Mrs. Lindijer left the house, I called Mary. She had no idea what to do either. She suggested that I should spend those two weeks at her house, but that was risky as Mary and Aad were involved in a lot of resistance work.

Then that warm August evening came. I'd been staying with Mary and Aad for ten days. We spent the last hours of the day on the porch, enjoying the cool of the evening. A couple of hours after we went to bed, the doorbell rang and there was banging on the door. We didn't open up quickly enough, so they kicked the door down. Three men stormed into the house. It was such a shock. I was completely distraught: It had all been for nothing. We were arrested and were allowed to grab only a few possessions. I was so terrified that I really needed to go to the bathroom. One of the men kept watch as I sat on the toilet, and then they took me to the truck.

In the Haagsche Veer prison, where they took us, there were another twenty-seven Jews. Mary and Aad had found shelter for all of them, so we must have been betrayed by someone who knew the resistance group and the addresses. Aad managed to exchange a few desperate words with his sister. Soon after that, he was executed, shot dead. Mary was released relatively quickly — they thought she was unimportant.

We were each given a bed with a straw mattress, a metal bowl, and a mug. I was in one big room together with some fellow prisoners. We sometimes used to do gymnastics and we made up songs about being in prison and about how much we wanted to go home.

The food in the prison was tolerable, we were allowed outside every other day, and the guards didn't mistreat us. We must have been easy prisoners. We rarely spoke about the immediate future. As long as we were in prison, our lives weren't at risk. In spite of everything, it felt good to use my real name again. It was only then that I realized how difficult it had been to keep using that other name. Bloeme Emden — I savored my own name.

One day we were told we were going to leave the prison. The Germans put us on a train to Westerbork. When we got there, we saw lots of people at the entrance to the camp, penned in with barbed wire. The first ones I saw were Margot and Anne Frank and their parents. They wanted to see if any of their family or friends were with us. I knew Margot and Anne from school. We were sent to Auschwitz at the same time. Fifty days later, Anne, Margot, and their mother were moved to Bergen-Belsen. I ended up in Liebau with fifty other Dutch women. A fellow prisoner from Auschwitz is still my best friend; she's ninety-four years old now.

After the war, my relationship with Freddy fell apart, much to the regret of his father in particular. Freddy kept checking up on me all the time. Where have you been? When will you be home? Why are you going out? I couldn't stand it. I'd been so powerless for years that I never wanted to feel locked up again.

Jack with his mother, summer 1939

JACK ELJON
Born in Amsterdam, June 2, 1937

I wasn't even three years old when the war began. I have very few memories of the time before that, but what I can remember is the feeling of warmth and security within our family. My father had a good job as a bank clerk, and we lived in the Rivierenbuurt district in the south of Amsterdam. My parents really loved me. We used to go on camping vacations in North Holland, and I can still remember sitting on my father's shoulders and playing with him on the beach, splashing about in the water and throwing a ball.

On the day war broke out, I woke up early. It was a beautiful, clear day, but there was the sound of airplanes all around. It made me feel anxious, so I went to my parents' bedroom. "Can I come in with you?" When I was snuggled in bed with them, my father said to my mother, "Lies, this is serious." He knew Jews were trying to escape from Germany, and he was convinced that Dutch Jews were in grave danger too.

As soon as we got up that morning, he went to pack our things and we headed for Schoorl, the village where we always went camping. So for me, the outbreak of war felt a bit like the start of a vacation. But we weren't going camping. This time we had a room in Aunt Trien and Uncle Willem's house instead of sleeping in a tent on their land. They had three children: an older son, a daughter, and a son around my age. I spent a lot of time playing with the younger son.

At first my father kept on going to work in Amsterdam as he had before. He usually came back to Schoorl on the train, but if there was no other option he slept in our house in Amsterdam.

The Germans started building bunkers in the dunes at the end of 1940. They thought the British would attack from the sea.

One day I was down on the beach, playing in the sand. When I glanced up, I saw a German soldier aiming his rifle at me, as if I were an animal. I ran in panic to Aunt Trien's house and cried my eyes out.

The Germans started coming through our yard and walking through the fields where Uncle Willem grew potatoes and vegetables. I looked like a typical little Jewish boy, so they thought it was becoming too dangerous for me. I had to leave.

My parents found a place for me at my aunt Greta's house in Haarlem. She was my father's sister. I was allowed to stay there because she was married to a non-Jewish man and so they weren't about to be deported. On the day I left, my mother went with me to the station. I had to say good-bye to her at the train. Another woman was taking me to Haarlem. "You need to go now," my mother said. "Or it's only going to be worse." She had to force herself to let me leave, and then she turned around and walked away. My parents soon went into hiding too, but in a different place.

Aunt Greta made me very welcome. Her eldest daughter, Rietje,[20] was particularly fond of me. Rietje often used to take me to the hairdresser's where she worked. I used to love going with her. Rietje was seventeen and too young to be a mother herself, but old enough to play mother. I enjoyed all of the attention.

One day the neighbors came by. My aunt knew they were members of the NSB, but they still used to talk to each other. "That Jewish child in your house has to go," they said. "There's

20. Pronounced "REET-chuh."

going to be a search tomorrow." But where could I go? My aunt had no idea what to do. So the neighbors said, "Bring him round to ours." Their house wouldn't be searched, because they were members of the party.

The evening before the search, my aunt Greta lifted me over the fence. It was a tall fence and she had to lift me up above her head. "Have you got him?" I heard her ask.

"Yes, just give him a little push." So she did, and I fell a short way, but they caught me on the other side. Those neighbors might have been collaborators, but they were good to me. I stayed in their house for three or four days until it was safe again at Aunt Greta's.

At the end of 1941, when the anti-Jewish measures were getting worse and worse, my aunt and uncle decided that it would be safer for me to stay elsewhere. "You have to leave," Aunt Greta said one day.

"Am I going to my mommy?"

"No," said my aunt. "But where you're going now will be a better place for you. And you'll have a fine time with the people you're staying with."

A lady from the resistance took me on the train to Zeist. Aunt Greta had made me promise that I would never say my own name. "From now on, you're called Henkie Mulder," she had said. I remembered what she said very well.

It was a long walk from the station to my new house in Zeist. As soon as I saw her, I realized that my new foster mother, Aunt Da, was old, much older than I thought she'd be. I must have been imagining the same kind of family that I'd stayed with in Haarlem. But Aunt Da was no Aunt Greta. And her daughters, Ali and Beppie, were nothing like my cousins.

I was in Zeist for eighteen months, until the end of 1943. It was a really miserable time. I slept badly, ate badly, and was often beaten. When I couldn't sleep, they hit me. When I didn't want to eat, they hit me. Whenever I said, "I want my mommy," they hit me.

It started early in the morning. I was awake every day at six. I didn't want to eat breakfast then, which made them very unhappy. They were doing their best to provide food for me, and I wouldn't eat it. The harder they hit me, the more stubbornly I refused to eat. It was a vicious circle: I was mean to them, and they were mean to me.

Jack's hiding place in Zeist, at #52 Van der Merschlaan (present-day photograph)

They would slap my face, and they used to whack me hard on the back with coat hangers too. As they were hitting me, I would shout out, "I want my mommy!"

"Well, your mommy isn't here," they yelled back, and hit me some more.

"So where is my mommy?"

"She's not here, and she's not coming either."

"Then I want to go to Aunt Greta's."

"Well, you can't."

And then I just started up again, "Where's my mother? I want my mommy, my mommy, my mommy." And they would start hitting me again. Ali was the worst. If I've ever hated anyone in my life, it was her. Beppie was occasionally a little gentler. "Leave him now," she'd say. "He's had enough of a beating."

Whatever food they put in front of me, I wouldn't eat it. To force me to eat something, two of the women would hold my arms tight while the other pinched my nose shut. As I gasped for air, one of them would stuff the food into my mouth. Then they would clamp my jaw shut. But I still didn't chew, and as soon as they let go of my chin, I spat the food back out. And then they would stuff it back in. If I finally did end up swallowing something, I sometimes vomited. They used to force the vomit back into my mouth as well.

One day they said, "Fine. If you don't want to eat, then don't eat." So I didn't eat for five days until they couldn't keep it up any longer, and they put food in front of me again. I had won.

I cried myself to sleep every night. I used to sleep in a tiny attic room that was more like a closet. There was only a bed and a chair in the room.

I used to go to kindergarten, which was dangerous because I stood out among all those little blond children. I thought school was great, because at least it meant I was away from those women.

On June 2, 1943, it was my sixth birthday. I was allowed to have a party and invite eight children. In their own way, the three women tried to make something of my birthday, but I was unable to look forward to it or really enjoy it. My parents weren't there. The only good thing that could have happened in Zeist would have been if my mother and father had suddenly turned up.

Even after I turned six, I stayed on at kindergarten. Sometime in October 1943 I was called out of class one morning. "Henkie Mulder is to report to the principal." Immediately the thought shot through my mind that I wouldn't have to go back to those horrible women. Everything happened very quickly, and I hid in the big box on the front of a delivery bike that was waiting outside the school.

Someone had given me away. The neighbors across the street had seen the **SS**[21] going into our house, obviously looking for me. The whole neighborhood knew where I was; I didn't even have a hiding place. It was probably one of the other neighbors who had reported me.

Just as the neighbors spotted the SS going into the house, the baker's boy arrived. "Go straight to the school," they said to him. "That Jewish child has to get away. If they find him, it's not going to end well."

21. **SS** (*Schutzstaffel*): a paramilitary organization often seen as the most brutal division of Adolf Hitler's Nazi Party.

Jack during his stay in Zeist, 1943

I crouched inside the box on the front of his bike, in the section that was used to transport the bread, and he slammed down the lid. Darkness. I could tell from the bumps that he was cycling away, down the street and out of the village. After a while, I couldn't stand it any longer, so I carefully pushed the lid open a little way. The baker's boy reacted immediately. "That lid doesn't open until I say so," he said. And he banged it shut. So I was in the dark again.

Much later, maybe an hour, the lid opened a tiny way. The baker's boy propped it open and went on cycling. Through the gap, I could see cows grazing in a meadow. He brought me to a minister in Maarn, a nearby village, who later took me to another address.

After that, I stayed at a whole series of different addresses. Usually they moved me late in the evening, on a bike. I can only vaguely remember those journeys now: the darkness, the cold, the back of the bike. The people I stayed with for only one or two nights are just a vague memory too.

It went on like that until late in 1943, when I was taken to Deventer. To get there, I had to cross the bridge over the River IJssel. The Germans would only let small groups of people over the bridge at a fixed time every day.

So there I stood, with about twenty other people. I wasn't allowed to speak or to look around. I had to hold hands with a woman I didn't know, and I had to keep on walking. It was a fall day, and it was so chilly. I remember being absolutely terrified on that bridge.

When we reached the other side, we headed to a small Red Cross center. It was like stepping into a warm bath; I suddenly felt that I was welcome. A lady sat me on her lap and put her arms around me. I'd forgotten what that felt like.

I traveled around a lot before ending up in Friesland in summer 1944, on a farm a few miles from the village of Hommerts, where I stayed until the end of the war. The Langeraap family loved having me there. They had five children and a sixth was born while I was staying with them. All of them were blond with blue eyes.

I enjoyed being with the Langeraap family — as far as that was possible. They didn't beat me and they didn't force me to eat. There was enough food there even in the Hunger Winter of 1944. They had some cows, a few goats, and lots of land, where they grew potatoes. It must have been difficult for them, because I was in my own sad and weary little world, where I thought about my mother every day, constantly wondering why she had abandoned me.

I went to school in Hommerts. In 1944, that was downright dangerous. If you were caught as a Jew, they packed you straight off to the camps. To get to Hommerts, I first had to cross the canal by the farm in a boat and then walk forty-five minutes through the meadows. Luckily I never had to walk alone. There were another three local children who went to school in Hommerts. It was cold that winter and the icy wind blew right through me on the way to school. Although I couldn't stand the cold, I learned to skate in Friesland, which I really enjoyed.

My classmates were nice to me. I turned into a little Jewish boy who spoke **Frisian**.[22] In fact, I got so used to speaking Frisian that it was months after the war before I could speak actual Dutch again.

---

22. **Frisian**, or **West Frisian**: a language closely related to Dutch, which is spoken in the province of Friesland in the north of the Netherlands.

One time that winter, the Germans came to search the house. It was the beginning of 1945. We were prepared for it, and I had a hiding place ready in the attic of the farmhouse. A small space had been boarded off for me between the sloping roof and the floor, not much bigger than a gutter. It was a kind of crawl space and there was just enough room for me inside.

We saw the Germans coming on a boat. There were three of them. "You have to go," said my foster mother. "Quick! Up to the attic!" I immediately knew that I was in danger. It took them a while to reach us, because they had to tie up the boat at the landing stage first. I crawled into the space and wriggled my way between the planks and the roof. I was safely hidden away before the Germans reached the house.

They searched the entire house, including the attic. I could see their boots through the gaps in the planks as they walked past. I held my breath, but I knew they wouldn't find me because it would have seemed impossible for someone to hide in such a small space.

The men from the **Gestapo**[23] stayed on the farm for a while. They had something to drink, and then they left on the boat. The family fetched me from my hiding place an hour and a half later when they were certain the Germans weren't coming back.

When Friesland was liberated at the end of April, they said, "You can tell us your name now." I didn't say anything. "Go on. Tell us

---

23. **Gestapo**: the German secret police. Their main activity was tracking down the enemies of the German occupiers. The Gestapo then sent their "enemies" to concentration camps with no legal representation. They were known for torturing their prisoners.

what you're really called. The war's over now." But I'd promised my aunt in Haarlem that I would never say my name. They begged me, they hit me, they tried everything to make me tell them my name. "I don't know," I kept on saying. "I can't remember what my name is." But I thought to myself, My name's Jacky Eljon. I know that perfectly well.

After liberation, the people in Westerbork, where my mother had been taken in February 1945, were given lists of children who had survived the war. But my name was never on those lists, of course, because no one knew what I was really called. The Red Cross knew by then that there was a little boy in Hommerts who couldn't remember his name. So they organized a meeting with women from Westerbork whose children had disappeared. Most of them had been murdered in concentration camps.

Two days before my eighth birthday, a Red Cross nurse came to fetch me. She took me to Sneek, a small city north of Hommerts. It was a really long way. I rode on the back of her bike for about ten miles. We went to a school gym, where lots of stern-looking men and women were sitting around a table.

There was also a line of twenty chairs in the gym, with bald-headed women seated on them. I spotted my mother immediately, but I wasn't allowed to go to her; I had to start at number one. I walked past all of those women with their bristly scalps. The Germans had shaved their heads and now their hair was starting to grow back. Near the end of the line sat number seventeen: my mother. I jumped onto her lap. Finally, after four years, I was back with her again.

I never felt so close to her as in that room in Sneek. After we were reunited, we went back to Westerbork. She was staying in the officers' quarters, where the SS had been during the war. Now the roles were reversed and the German soldiers were in the sheds. My father was there with us too on that first night in Westerbork. He had taken up his job at the bank again but was working in Groningen for the time being, instead of in Amsterdam.

The first time he saw me, he fell on his knees and thanked the Lord for saving me. I thought he was acting really strangely, because I didn't know anything about Our Dear Lord. Later I found out that he'd picked up various Christian habits during his time in hiding, although he remained Jewish and was proud of it. At that moment, when I saw him down there on his knees, I thought he was crazy, even repulsive. He seemed nothing like my father from before the war, the man I'd longed to see.

We celebrated my eighth birthday, two days later, in Westerbork. I even got a present: a pen and eight pots of colored ink to draw with. But what I remember most clearly is wanting to have an egg. And I got one, too: a fried egg in a little pan. I ate my egg at the window of the officers' house where my mother was staying, with the Germans across the way, guarded by Dutch soldiers. And, as they stood there watching, I licked the pan. That was my revenge.

We stayed at Westerbork until we were allowed to return to Amsterdam. Everyone seemed happy that the war was over.

Later, though, it all turned sour. I couldn't forgive my parents for handing me over to strangers. I couldn't shake off the feeling

Onderduikerskaart   Registratienummer 6040

De gezamenlijke voormalige verzorgingsorganisaties van onderduikers te Amsterdam verklaren

dat .... *M. Elzon*

geboren *2 Juni 1937*   No. identiteitsbewijs *T.D. 866009*

tegenwoordig adres *Rhijndenstraat 48*

om principiele redenen ondergedoken is geweest

van *April 1942*   tot *5 Mei 1945*

Wij verzoeken alle overheidsinstellingen, bedrijven en organisaties op het gebied van hulpverlening, houder dezer behulpzaam te willen zijn.

ELCO—Oct. '45

Alleen geldig mits afgestempeld

Jack's hiding certificate. These documents were issued after the war to show that someone had gone into hiding. At the bottom it reads, *We call on all government institutions, companies, and welfare organizations to assist the holder of this card.*

that they'd abandoned me. There's no way a boy of four can understand the idea of being sent away for his own good. I would never, ever let any children of mine go into hiding alone, or hand them over to strangers.

That warm feeling I had as a little boy sitting on my father's shoulders was gone for good. I rejected my father. I didn't want to be on his lap. I didn't want to give him a kiss. I kept well away from him.

The Langeraap family from Friesland emigrated soon after the war, so I never had any further contact with them. But Aunt Da, Ali, and Beppie were still living in Zeist. My parents made me visit them and say thank you. I had to go see Aunt Da when I was ten, twelve, seventeen. She and her daughter Beppie even came to my wedding. I went on visiting her in the retirement home until she died. "She saved your life," my father always used to say whenever he dragged me there yet again. That's true. She saved my life. "And she ruined it too," I always used to add.

Rose-Mary Kahn, c. 1938

MY FATHER'S STORE

ROSE-MARY KAHN
Born in Amsterdam, July 6, 1925

During the first days of the war, we often talked about escaping. Initially my father wasn't at all enthusiastic about the idea. He didn't want to abandon his business. "Everything will turn out fine," he said.

"It won't turn out fine at all," my mother would reply. "We have to find a way to get out of here." She finally managed to persuade my father, and a few days later we went to the port at the town of IJmuiden. We hardly took anything with us. But we got there too late, and the boats were all full. So we went back home again, and I ran straight up to my bedroom to clean off some words I'd written on the windows. It was something like "Germans, go home!"

My father's clothing store was called Hirsch and it was very well-known in Amsterdam: Hirsch on Leidseplein, a major square in the city center. Before the war, people used to come to Hirsch from all over the Netherlands. Twice a year, the salesgirls would call the regular customers: "There's a new collection. Would you like to come in and see it?" It was a very fashionable store.

I understand that my father didn't want to leave: The business was very important to him. Running away felt like betraying the business he'd worked so hard to build up and the family he'd done it with.

Soon after the war broke out, in June or July 1940, my father's brother, who was also a member of the management at Hirsch, made an anti-German speech at the store. When he told us at home that he was going to do it, my mother tried to stop him. "Arnold, you mustn't do that. There's no point. It'll only turn out badly." But Uncle Arnold did it anyway. He gave his speech in front of the entire staff, some of whom supported the Germans.

Hirsch & Co., c. 1947

The next day, the entire management was arrested: Uncle Arnold, my father, and the co-owner, Robert Berg. This was right at the beginning of the war, and my father and Robert Berg had said nothing themselves, so they were released after three weeks. A few months later, when the measures against Jews became stricter, there's no way that would have happened.

My mother went to the headquarters of the German secret police to try to get Uncle Arnold out. She was in the lion's den, and that was obviously a huge risk. I should add that my mother was a very beautiful woman, and she made quite an impression on the Germans. One of the men even said, *"Sind sie sicher, dass Sie Jüdin sind?"* (Are you certain you're Jewish?)

My mother replied, *"Hundert Prozent sicher."* (One hundred percent certain.) There was little they could do to help her, but strangely they didn't arrest her and they just let her go home. Uncle Arnold was sent to the Buchenwald concentration camp, where he was *"auf der Flucht erschossen"* (shot during an escape attempt) that same summer. The Germans often used that excuse. It actually meant that the person had been murdered.

A few weeks later, still in the summer of 1940, someone rang our doorbell at ten o'clock in the evening. My mother's brother, who was living with us at the time, went to see who was there. He shouted through the door and asked who it was.

"We have a letter for Mr. Kahn," came the answer.

"Just put it through the door," said my uncle.

"Can't do that," they said. "It's too big."

So my uncle opened the door. They pushed their way into the house, shooting as they came. "It's a raid!" my uncle yelled.

My mother immediately locked the door of the front room. I was in the bathroom off the hallway, so I had heard everything, and I didn't dare move a muscle. My father, who knew where I was, wanted to come to me. "No, no!" my mother cried. "They won't do anything to her. It's you they're after."

After about five minutes, I started screaming. I was terrified. They smashed the windows in the bathroom door. I put my hands over my eyes. This is the end, I thought, as the glass shattered and fell all around me. Now they're going to drag me out of here and shoot me dead. They saw me standing there, in the corner of the bathroom. I was fifteen, but I was pretty small for my age. They did nothing, just as Mother had predicted.

They shot everything in the hallway to pieces, and then they ran back out of the house and it was silent.

That raid had a huge impact on us. We really thought they were going to murder my father — and those men were Dutch, not Germans. The next day, the police came, the Dutch police, but they just walked around the place for a while and picked up a couple of bullets. There was nothing else they could do. It was over; it was all over for us. I felt so powerless. No one did a thing to help us.

A few days later, we went to stay with the Boissevain family. They were Hirsch customers who had a hotel in Beekbergen, in the countryside. We stayed there for a few weeks until we felt that things had calmed down a bit and we could return to Amsterdam.

My father went back to work. It was pretty quiet for months, until one afternoon sometime in 1941, when my parents were visiting a half-Jewish friend who lived around the corner from us. The Germans must have seen my parents go into the house. According to the German **race laws**,[24] someone who was half-Jewish didn't count as a Jew. And it was forbidden for Jews to visit non-Jews, so my parents were arrested. My father was first sent to prison in Amsterdam and then to Westerbork. My mother dug her heels in. "I am not going," she said. "I have two children at home, two young children. I refuse to go." It may sound incredible, but it somehow confused the Germans. And so they let her go home. My mother was a difficult woman, and she used to complain about the most trivial things, but the war brought out the

---

24. **race laws**: three racist, anti-Jewish laws that Germany introduced on September 15, 1935, which meant that Jewish citizens no longer had any civil rights. These laws were later responsible for Jews being systematically persecuted and murdered.

best in her: She had to fight for her family, and she realized that other people could rely on her.

The major raids began in 1942. The situation became very dangerous for us. Anyone could be picked up at any moment. But we didn't dare go into hiding, because we were scared that they would send my father to "the East" as punishment. At the time we didn't know exactly what that meant, of course, but it was clear that it was a terrible fate.

Thanks to our neighbor, Mr. Saarloos, we were able to stick it out in our own house for a long time. When the Germans no longer allowed Jews to go shopping, he did it for us. There were some NSB members living across the street, so he threw the groceries over the fence at the back of the house.

Saarloos, who worked for the police, warned us one day: "The Germans are coming for you tonight, because they want your house." We had no choice. We moved immediately and went to stay with Ang van Slooten, a Hirsch employee who did a great deal to help us. We were able to stay there for only a few weeks, as Ang's husband found sheltering three people very difficult. My mother was scared someone would betray us, and so she decided we should leave.

We moved in with our former babysitter next. We had a really close relationship with her. I was only three months old when she came to work for the family. But her husband was also eager for us to leave. After a week, we went back to Ang's, where Mr. Kuurman, a former teacher from my elementary school who had joined the resistance, came to fetch us. He was to take us on the train to Doornspijk, a village on the Veluwe River.

We were terrified that we would be spotted at Centraal Station in Amsterdam. My brother lifted his suitcase onto his shoulder to make it impossible for the ticket clerk to see his face. Oh no, I thought, that's only going to attract more attention. On the train, Mr. Kuurman sat in a different car. If we got caught, he wasn't with us.

We never saw Mr. Kuurman again, but Ang knew where we were, and she later brought my father to the place where we were hiding in Doornspijk. He escaped from Westerbork with the help of a friend of Ang's who was a foodwaste collector.

In Westerbork, there was a roll call twice a day. The prisoners were made to stand in orderly lines, and the Germans would check their lists to make sure everyone was still there. My mother had written my father a coded letter saying that he should escape before the evening roll call by crawling under a fence and hiding until the foodwaste man could pick him up.

My father waited until the new moon, so that it would be really dark. Then he made his escape, as arranged, before the evening roll call, and ran to the agreed hiding place. As he was waiting for the foodwaste man, a patrol of Germans and military police came past. One of the military policemen saw my father lying there. They looked each other straight in the eye, but the man didn't say a word.

The food collector found my father, hid him under the peelings, drove back into the camp, and then left Westerbork as usual by the main entrance, past the guards. Ang went to fetch my father the next day and took him on the train and on a bicycle to the place where we were hiding.

●　　●　　●

The farmhouse in Doornspijk had two large rooms. In one of them, the upstairs room, the Van Zeeburg family used to drink coffee on Sundays, and we spent the whole week in the other room. We hardly ever went outside, mainly because my brother thought it was far too dangerous. Sometimes my mother and I didn't listen, and we used to sneak out to the field behind the farm. That often caused arguments, but we were too dependent on one another to allow them to go on for too long — and, to be honest, arguing helped to combat the boredom.

My mother and I slept in the big room, while my father and my brother slept in the attic. There were two other people hiding with the Van Zeeburg family, a German-Jewish mother and her son. The son didn't look at all Jewish. He even used to go out and work as a farmhand. We had very little to do. We used to play cards and read a lot. We had lists of books from the library in Nunspeet, and we marked on the list what we wanted to read. Then the Van Zeeburg family would fetch the books for us, together with all kinds of religious books that they wanted to read themselves. After the war, one of the library staff said she had suspected people were hiding with the Van Zeeburg family. "They suddenly started asking for very different books."

The family had a grandmother who was in her seventies. The farmer, Beert, was around thirty. He was engaged. Then there was an unmarried female farmer in her fifties and an unmarried half sister. Their married sisters used to come visit too, and they all knew that we were Jews in hiding.

The Van Zeeburgs were not in it for the money at all, but of course we all needed money to live. During our stay, we sold my mother's fur coat and gave the money to the family. After the war, my parents gave the family a horse cart and a bell for the church tower. My brother requested a **Yad Vashem medal**[25] for them, and they received one.

My brother made a hatch in the attic that opened into the empty space between the floor and the ceiling beneath. No one could see it because the saw cuts were exactly in the gaps between the planks. We used that space a few times, whenever we heard someone come in through the back door or the stable door, which were nearly always open.

It always turned out to be a false alarm — until one afternoon when someone from the resistance warned us that German soldiers were going from farm to farm, looking for British airmen who had been shot down. We raced to the attic and climbed through the hole and crouched down in there, listening as the Germans came into the house and searched every room, floor by floor. One time they actually walked over our hiding place. I was scared to death. That hiding place saved our lives.

One day in April 1945, our neighbor Hannes, who was in the resistance, came by and said, "The Canadians are in Elburg." My father flew out of the house, with my brother and me right behind him. We had been out there talking for just a moment when we noticed some movement in the straw in the nearby barn. Then two German soldiers came out of the straw, dressed in uniform and fully armed.

"Back inside!" shouted my brother. "Back inside!"

---

25. **Yad Vashem medal**: an Israeli medal to honor non-Jews who risked their lives to help Jews during the Holocaust.

"We're not going anywhere," said my father. "We've been liberated."

The German soldiers wanted to surrender, but that wasn't so easy. The Canadians had already reached Nunspeet, three and a half miles away, but they hadn't yet made it to Doornspijk, the village where we were in hiding. Farmer Beert went to Nunspeet. A few hours later, he returned with a British officer, who disarmed the Germans. After all those years, it was the most wonderful moment.

Almost immediately after the entire country had been liberated, my father and my brother returned to Amsterdam to organize housing for us. We couldn't go back to our house on De Lairessestraat. It was full of policemen, and they weren't ready to leave. The authorities weren't particularly helpful. It was more

The Kahn family just after the liberation, at the Zeeburg family farm

than a year before we could go back to our own home. The few Jews who returned were seen as an administrative nuisance.

Hirsch had been stripped so bare that my father had to start all over again. And that's exactly what he did. He opened a store on Kalverstraat at first, one of the main shopping streets in Amsterdam. A few years later, we returned to Leidseplein. But it was never as successful as it had been before the war.

That period in hiding was terrible. It was the worst time of my life. Nothing that has happened since has done anything to change that.

I wanted to move on, but it's been impossible. A few weeks ago, I had to apply for a new passport, as the old one had expired. My cleaning lady said, "Why don't you just get one of those identity cards? They're cheaper and you never go on vacation outside Europe these days anyway. A passport's no good to you."

"Yes, it is," I replied. "I need to be able to escape."

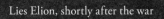
Lies Elion, shortly after the war

THANK GOODNESS
THEY WERE ALL BOYS

LIES ELION
Born in Amsterdam, February 28, 1931

My father was a diamond merchant. There were a lot of Jews working in the diamond industry. My parents also had plenty of Jewish friends and acquaintances, but my father thought it was very important for us to be just like everyone else. He didn't celebrate Jewish holidays, and he didn't talk about Judaism. In fact, I didn't know anything about Judaism until one day a friend of mine said, "Hey, you're Jewish, aren't you?"

"Jewish, Jewish . . . What does that mean?"

"My parents think you're Jewish."

So I went to my parents and asked them.

"That's right," they said. "You're Jewish."

"And what's Jewish?"

"We're Jewish and our parents were Jewish and so on. So you're Jewish too."

I still didn't understand.

We could tell that the war had broken out from the plumes of smoke above Schiphol, the airport near Amsterdam. Our house was full of panic, threat, fear. What were we going to do? Although he was naturally pessimistic, my father discouraged any reports of bad news, and he got furious when someone said that the war might go on for a long time.

On May 15, we attempted to escape to America by ship. Someone stopped us on the way to the port and said, "The last boat has already gone. You should turn around." My mother was actually relieved. She found it hard to leave her belongings behind.

At the beginning of the war, not long after the Netherlands had surrendered, a boy from our neighborhood said, "I can't play marbles with you anymore because you're Jewish. My mother doesn't like it." I was really upset. My parents thought it was terrible. They went to speak to the neighbors, and I never played marbles with that boy again. "Make sure you stay away from him," said my mother. They never spoke about it again after that.

In 1941, all Jewish children were made to leave their schools and go to a special Jewish school. I didn't feel at home there among all those children with traditional Jewish backgrounds. I couldn't read Hebrew, and I knew nothing about Jewish holidays.

To learn more about Judaism, I went to a special class every week where I studied Hebrew. In my first lesson they told me, "You're holding the book wrong. Books in Hebrew start at the back." Every week, in the days leading up to my Hebrew class, I used to feel completely miserable. I was the odd one out wherever I went, whether it was with Jews or non-Jews.

More and more children disappeared, including my best friend, Gertie van Berg, with whom I walked to the Jewish school every day. In 1942, I received a farewell postcard from her: "We're on our way to Poland."

My sister, Selly, was seven and a half years older than me, and she soon realized that we were in serious danger because we were Jews. As we were washing the dishes one day, she said, "I'll never let them catch me, because I'm dead if that happens. I'm going to do whatever it takes to keep out of their clutches." And then she said, "If we survive and you have children, you should name one of them after me, and I'll do the same. So my daughter will be called Lize Marie, and if you have a daughter you can call her Selly." I must have given her a funny look — I was only ten at the time.

The threat was coming closer. But our father didn't want to go into hiding. He didn't want to put other people at risk.

A lot of Jews were made to move to Amsterdam, so Uncle Dolf, my father's brother, came to live with us, along with his wife and two daughters. One day, Uncle Dolf was told to report to the headquarters of the German security police. He didn't go. I noticed that he gave everyone a kiss at breakfast. Then he went out and jumped into the river. His suicide left a huge impression on me. Everyone at home was devastated.

In June 1943, there was a roundup in our neighborhood. The Germans announced their arrival through a loudspeaker. Then some men in uniforms forced their way into our house. We were taken on the tram to the sports field at Olympiaplein. It was only a short ride. There was a woman in front of me with a baby on her lap in a travel crib. "Look," said my mother. "Such a little one. How terrible that they're deporting even babies."

We waited on the sports field for what seemed like forever. Finally they took us to Muiderpoort train station. There were lots of Germans there, walking up and down the platforms, with their guns and dogs. Suddenly my sister said, "Listen, Lies. I'm about to make a run for it. I'll dash between the train carriages, and then I'll disappear. Don't say anything to Mom and Dad, not a word. You mustn't tell them until the train has started moving."

I was scared to death. She's going to get shot, I thought. I'm going to hear a gunshot at any moment. But nothing happened. They made us get on the train. It wasn't a regular train car but the kind that's normally used to transport animals. We just stood there, waiting and waiting. Then my mother started to panic, "Where's Sel? Where's Sel? Lies, do you know where Sel is?" I didn't tell her Sel was trying to escape until the train started moving. I found out later that she'd managed to hide behind a platform. Then she went to her boyfriend Mark's house. Later, in Westerbork, where the train was heading, we received the news that Sel and Mark had gotten married. We knew then that she must have gone into hiding. If you wanted to go into hiding together, you had to be married or you'd never find a family that would take you in.

Westerbork transit camp, c. 1943. On the left, a train carrying deportees has arrived.

When we arrived at Westerbork, we were taken to a large room, where lots of people were crammed in together. My father was worried that they'd find the diamonds he'd hidden on himself. He thought children wouldn't be searched, so he asked me to hide the diamonds in my underwear. I didn't want to do it, and I thought it was a really strange thing to ask. I have no idea what he actually did with the diamonds.

We were in Westerbork for three weeks. Then we heard that we had to go back to Amsterdam. I had no idea what was going on. We'd left in a cattle car and now we were returning to Amsterdam on a regular train. And my father didn't explain to me that we were going back because he'd been placed on a list of important diamond merchants. That meant he'd been given a *Sperre*, a temporary exemption from deportation. He rarely explained anything to me. I became angry about that later, when I had children of my own.

"Why did you never tell me anything?" I asked him.

"You were too young to understand. That's why I didn't tell you anything," he replied.

My sister was in hiding with Mark, her husband. They were living at a friend's house but, after just a few weeks, the friend said, "You'll have to leave because we're going on vacation." They quickly looked for another place to stay. Mark's mother found somewhere, but the address proved to be unreliable, and someone gave them away to the Germans. They ended up in the Hollandsche Schouwburg, where the Germans found our details in her address book. So my father, mother, and I were picked up again, because the exemption from deportation was automatically withdrawn if someone in your family had been labeled as a criminal, which happened to people who were caught trying to escape or hide. We were taken to the Hollandsche Schouwburg as well. Like many other children, I ended up in the kindergarten on the other side of the street. Some people from the resistance tried to help me go into hiding. They pulled me through the hedge into the school next door and someone said, "We have a good address for you." I put up a fight. "I don't want to go!" I yelled. I was scared that my parents would be punished for my escape. The next day, when I went to see my parents during visiting hour, I found out that they knew about the escape attempt.

"Prisoners" in the yard at the Hollandsche Schouwburg, 1942

"What's wrong with you?" they said. "You could have gotten away, couldn't you?"

"But I didn't want to go."

As they were "criminal offenders," Sel and Mark were kept far away from my parents inside the Hollandsche Schouwburg, somewhere on a balcony on the third floor. We only got to speak to her once. When she was in the sickroom with a bladder infection, the Germans gave us permission to visit her briefly. She told us that someone had offered to help her escape and that, like me, she'd refused because she was scared it would put others in danger. So both of us had chosen not to escape. Soon after that, she was deported with Mark — first to Westerbork, and later to Auschwitz.

My parents and I made it out of the Hollandsche Schouwburg. I still don't know how. There was probably some bribery involved. When we got back home, the tension between my parents increased. My mother thought my father should have done more for Sel, that there must have been something he could have done. She thought he'd waited too long.

On the morning of September 29, I was walking to school at around eight thirty. Halfway there, I bumped into Mrs. Van Woerkom, who had been renting a room in our house. She was delighted to see me, and she hugged me really tight. "Lies, Lies, are you still here? There's been a raid in your neighborhood." She ran back home with me. It turned out that the Germans had missed our house. They'd simply forgotten about us.

She practically had to force my parents to go into hiding. "You absolutely have to leave. Now! You can't stay here even one more night." She knew a woman called Mrs. De Swaan who lived on Stadionkade, and was sheltering a number of Jewish children. She went to her and told her it was an emergency.

Mrs. De Swaan said we could go to her house right away, but that we couldn't stay there, because she was expecting more Jewish children. So Mrs. De Swaan got in touch with Uncle Hannes. My mother had such a terrible shock when Hannes Boogaard came to the house, with his scruffy clothes and his stubbly chin. The plan was for him to take me on the bus to a hiding place. "I'm not sending my daughter away with him," said my mother. "That's simply not going to happen."

"I won't sit next to her on the bus," said Uncle Hannes. "I'll sit at the back, and Lies will be right up front. I won't have anything to do with her."

I went with Uncle Hannes. I was leaving home for the first time — and I found it very difficult. I was really worried about my parents too.

At Hannes Boogaard's farm, he gave me the place of honor. "You come and sit here beside me." He comforted me and tried to cheer me up. Later he showed me a whole bed full of children, all of them in hiding. "You see why you can't stay here?"

Uncle Hannes's son Teun took me to another address nearby. When the people came to the door, they were really indignant. "Who's this you've brought?" they said. "We asked for a girl of at least seventeen, didn't we? We want a housemaid, not a little girl."

"I'm sure she'll be perfectly capable of helping around the house," said Teun.

Although I'd never done any housework before, I played along. "I'm good at peeling potatoes and good at cleaning," I said. They let me stay. I was given a tiny little bedroom and had no contact with the only other child in the house. They made me work as their maid and they really made me work hard: In addition to my daily chores, they wanted me to dust and wax all of the furniture once a week. That meant that everything had to be moved — and it was all so heavy! I used to cry myself to sleep every night.

My only comfort was my friendship book, which accompanied me throughout the whole war. It starts with happy little poems and pictures, when life was still good. My uncle was the first to write in the book, in January 1940, a few days after I received it. He was followed by other uncles, aunts, and friends, all the way up to the middle of 1942. The poems were nothing special. Boys would write something like, "Oh, say, take a look, my name's in your book." One Jewish girl wrote, "To every child that is born the Lord gives a guiding light, to lead them and to comfort in the darkness of the night." They were clichés that we copied from one another, but during the war I became very fond of them.

One day someone from the resistance came to our door. "The child has to leave. Right now. They're doing a roundup." With my apron still on, I jumped onto the back of his bike. When we reached the town of Hillegom, he said, "I have a surprise for you." He'd taken me to the place where my parents were staying, with the Ten Hoope family.

"Listen," said Mrs. Ten Hoope, "the child can't stay here. All I have is a place in the attic, but there are rats and mice up there."

"I'd rather put up with mice and rats than have to leave," I said. My parents agreed. They wouldn't let me go. Upstairs in the attic, I could constantly hear scuttling noises, but I wasn't scared. I was just relieved that I could stay there and be with my parents.

We spent most of our time upstairs. Occasionally we were allowed downstairs. When there were unexpected visitors, the family used to chase us into an old-fashioned closet under the stairs, where we stood and waited, huddled closely together, until the visitor left, which was often a long time. It was pretty cramped in there. What was really amazing was that their little boy, who wasn't even three years old at the time, used to call to us, "Uncle Co, Aunt Bert, you can come out now." He was so small, but that little boy still knew exactly when to keep quiet and when he could tell us to come back out.

We had to leave that place too. The family sold homegrown tobacco, which was absolutely forbidden. They thought someone had given them away, and so the police might arrive at the door at any moment. We went to a new address in Hillegom, which we had to leave in a hurry when someone was arrested for smuggling and our address was found in his diary. Panic! There was no new place for us to go. We didn't even have false identity cards, but everyone called me Lies Evers, and I wasn't allowed to say my own name.

In desperation, my father just walked into a hotel, where he explained the situation to the hotel owner and asked for a room. The man let us stay, on the condition that we behaved like regular hotel guests and didn't hide away in our room. So we ate in the dining room, like everyone else. It was all going fine, until one day an SS officer sat down at the table next to ours. We were so anxious that we could hardly eat a bite. We didn't dare look at him, but just stared down at our plates. Nothing happened. He just paid, and he left. I'm still proud of my father for having the courage to go into that hotel.

Around ten days later, the resistance found a new place for us, with Mrs. Wisse, a widow with two daughters who were in high school. I used to borrow books from them so that I could read and learn something. Mrs. Wisse was a seamstress, and my mother used to help her with hems and seams. She spent every day in Mrs. Wisse's sewing room, altering countless hems and seams.

In the evenings we were allowed out into the yard for some fresh air. We used to walk around in circles for exercise and to stay warm. There was a large container of rabbit food in the middle of the yard and, as he walked past, my father would run his hand through the food and take some. "Mmmm," he used to say. "What a delicious meal!" He made a big joke of it, but he was simply hungry.

One day, when we were in our room upstairs, my father said, "Take this piece of paper and keep it somewhere safe. There's an address on it for a man from the resistance. We're going to hand ourselves in."

I was astonished. "What's going to happen to me?"

"You can stay here. You're in good hands. We're going to turn ourselves in, so we can be in Westerbork with Sel."

I headed downstairs with the piece of paper in my hand. Halfway down the stairs, I started screaming and Mrs. Wisse came flying, "Whatever's wrong?"

I told her what was going on and handed her the piece of paper. She was furious with my parents. She really yelled at them. She finished by saying, "This is not going to happen!"

Although my parents didn't hand themselves in, I've never been able to get over that incident. How could they even think of leaving me behind?

During the war, I clung to the idea that Sel would escape again, because everything had gone so well for her the first time, back at Muiderpoort Station. She was out there somewhere, I thought. Maybe she'd found a place to hide in Germany. "I'll never let them catch me," she'd said.

My parents argued a lot during the months at Mrs. Wisse's. My mother still blamed my father for not having done enough for Sel, and my father felt that wasn't fair.

"I can't take this arguing any longer," Mrs. Wisse said one day. We had to leave. She thought it was becoming too dangerous. That's what she said. In reality, there must have been another reason, because after we left she took in another Jewish family.

We moved in with the Pos family next, where some other people were already hiding. That was nice, particularly for my father, because he could discuss the war with them. This was the winter of 1944. There was a famine, but there was also hope that the war was coming to an end.

We stayed there for a number of weeks, until Mrs. Pos said to my mother, "There's something I need to say to you. This is difficult, but I think you'd better find another place to stay."

"Why?" said my mother.

"It's your husband. He always looks so gloomy. We can't stand the sight of his miserable face any longer."

That was a real blow for my father. It was impossible for him to change his face. The gloominess was all part of his character, and it was also the situation, of course. He couldn't stand having to hide away like that.

But my mother had a bright idea. One afternoon, Mrs. Rooyakkers had come to visit, a friendly woman who lived three or four houses down. We knew she wasn't a collaborator, because we'd been allowed to talk to her. My mother went to visit her. "I have a strange request," she said, "and you must give me an honest answer. We've been told to leave, and we don't know what to do."

"Fine. You can come to our house. Our doors are open wide. But we have five children. Come upstairs with me. I'll show you our supply of beans."

She took my mother upstairs. It wasn't much food for so many people. "This is all we have to get by with, for all of us. It's all the food we have. Is that all right with you?"

We moved in with them. The first night, Mr. and Mrs. Rooyakkers let my parents sleep in their bedroom. "You must get a good night's sleep," they said.

When I visited Cor Rooyakkers many years later in the retirement home, I asked her why she took us in when there was so little food in the house. "Lots of children had measles at the time," she said. "And I thought: If I take in that family, then perhaps God will see that my children don't catch measles."

It was a simple laborer's house, with the dunes on one side and the other side looking out over the bulb fields where the flowers grew in the springtime. We ate a lot of mashed bulbs while we were there.

My father hardly ever went outside, but when the beans finally ran out, he took a wheelbarrow to a nearby farm. He let me go with him. He swapped his wedding rings for a load of wheat. We came back to the house with a full wheelbarrow, and the Rooyakkers family was delighted. My father was pleased that he could do something to help them for once.

Gradually the threat lessened and my parents allowed me to play in the dunes with the local children. "Doesn't Lies have a funny walk!" they said the first time I went out. "And she can't run at all."

"Is that any surprise?" said Aunt Cor. "She's spent years indoors. This is the first time she's run."

My father started teaching me. He taught me French and English. He wanted me to go to a good school after the war, the Amsterdams Lyceum. A math teacher even used to visit the house to help me prepare.

When, one morning, news of the liberation reached us, my father walked in his slippers to De Zilk, a nearby village. He couldn't believe what he'd heard. He saw the notices nailed to the trees that said we'd been liberated, and he brought one home with him. An hour later, we were standing by the fireplace, and he said, "Lies, from now on, you're not called Lies Evers anymore. Your name is Lies Elion."

After those first joyful days, we went back on the boat to Amsterdam. As we heard more stories about the camps, we began to realize that Sel and her husband would never return.

When I heard the newspaper arrive, I used to sneak downstairs to see if there was any news about the camps. If I found anything, I would tear out the page and hide it. "Hey," my mother would say, "there's a page missing." I didn't want her to read about the horrors.

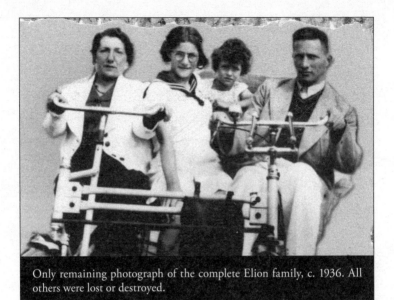

Only remaining photograph of the complete Elion family, c. 1936. All others were lost or destroyed.

On Friday evenings, friends or the occasional relative who had also survived the war would come visit. There was always a strange atmosphere in the house on those occasions. We didn't dare speak out loud about what had happened. Women would whisper behind their handkerchiefs about who had come back from the East and who hadn't.

I often tried to make my parents feel better and to be a replacement for my sister. But it was impossible. Sometimes I used to say, "Look, you've still got me."

My mother's reaction was, "You don't say to someone whose leg has been amputated, 'Just be happy you still have the other one,' do you?" She must have said that four or five times.

Nothing was allowed in our house anymore. No parties, no

Sinterklaas.[26] My only cousin on my mother's side felt so sorry for me that he bought me a present once. He thought he should tell my parents before he gave it to me. "I'm coming to visit at Sinterklaas," he said, "to bring by a few presents."

They gave him an earful. "We don't celebrate Sinterklaas, and we don't want you here."

At the New Year, they went to bed extra early and left me on my own. I went in to wish them a happy New Year at midnight, but they threw me out of their room: "We don't do that anymore."

I had five children myself. Thank goodness they were all boys. Whenever I was pregnant, I couldn't help remembering what my sister had said — that we would name our daughters after each other if we survived the war. My mother couldn't have coped with a granddaughter called Selly. It would have been really hard for me too.

Much later I made an imitation friendship book to help me process my wartime experiences. I wrote poems about the happy months of the prewar period and then the dark years of the war and how it really felt to go into hiding. I wrote about the sadness after the war but also how delighted my parents were later with my children and what a great comfort that was for me. I felt that I had been able to make their lives a little better by having children. The book has now become a sort of family history in verse.

---

26. Sinterklaas: a festival held in the Netherlands on December 5–6, when Saint Nicholas (Sinterklaas) visits the country, and families and friends exchange presents.

Selly's drawing in Lies's friendship book. The page facing it remains blank.

It was a drawing my sister did that prompted me to create that book. She decided that she wanted to write something in my friendship book. She'd already done a drawing on one page and she was going to write a poem on the other page. She never had the chance. The drawing was a portrait of me. She asked me, "Liesje, do you think it looks like you?" and I wrote those words beneath the picture. But I left the other page blank, because that's how it has to be. I can't finish it for her.

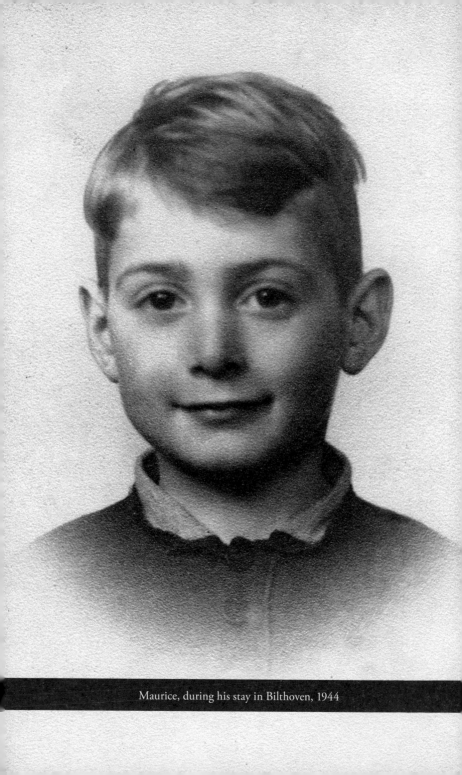

Maurice, during his stay in Bilthoven, 1944

WHERE ARE THE JACKETS?

MAURICE MEIJER
Born in Amsterdam, June 5, 1937

After the war we moved into a new home in Amsterdam. We found some documents in the apartment belonging to a Mr. Maas, a fanatical NSB member who had lived there during the war. My mother took the papers to the **PRA**,[27] which was set up after the war to serve justice on Dutch people who had collaborated with the Germans. Maas was sentenced to a few months in prison.

But when he got out, Maas rented a room from our neighbor downstairs. Lots of apartments back then had an extra attic room at the top of the house. And that was the room that the neighbor gave to Maas. So, to reach his room, he had to go up our stairs. When our mother heard him coming up the stairs the first time, she went out and said to him, "You will not walk up my staircase, because I'm not planning to clean up after any NSB member. There's an ax waiting for you up here. If you walk up my stairs one more time I'm going to bash your brains in."

Mr. Maas complained to the police. A few days later, a detective rang our doorbell. "Is it true that you threatened your neighbor with an ax?"

"Yes," said my mother. "Look, there it is. I'm going to bash his brains in if he walks up my stairs. I'm not cleaning up any NSB member's dusty footprints."

And the detective replied, "If you promise me that you'll take that ax away, I'll make sure he stops using your stairs."

And that's what happened. He moved into a room inside the neighbor's apartment instead. He never walked up our stairs again. My mother and he sometimes used to cross on other parts

27. **PRA:** *Politieke Recherche Afdeling* (Political Investigation Department)

of the staircase, but she would never step out of his way. He was the one who had to stand aside.

This was after the war. I don't remember much from before the war. But I was born in 1937, so I was only three when the war broke out. My father, Salomon Meijer, was a tram conductor in Amsterdam. The Germans immediately laid off the Jews who worked for the city, so he was one of the first to lose his job. They sent him to work in the forest near Staphorst. A group of them was allowed to come home to visit for a few days, but some of them escaped and went into hiding, so the Germans sent a second group to Westerbork as punishment. My father was part of that group.

Before her marriage, my mother, Ester Jas, had worked as a cap seamstress. After my father left, which I don't remember, our family had no income. My mother's eldest brother probably gave us some money now and then. My mother had foresight: We went into hiding before they really started to go after the Jews here. We first hid with my aunt, Lena Talhuizen, and we slept in her attic — but that must have become too dangerous because we weren't there for long. My brother and I had gone into hiding without our mother. I can't remember saying good-bye to her. She stayed in various places in the city, working for the resistance, until she got caught.

They took her to the headquarters of the *Sicherheitsdienst*, the German intelligence agency. At first they suspected her only of working for the resistance, until a former neighbor of ours surfaced. She told them that my mother was Jewish and mentioned in passing that she also had two Jewish sons who had gone into hiding. They mistreated my mother very badly in an attempt to find out where we were hiding. But she was truly unable to tell them anything, because she knew nothing about where we were.

They later transported her to Vught, a concentration camp near Den Bosch. On the way there, she passed through Centraal Station in Utrecht, where she spotted me in the distance, purely by chance. Later still, she was sent to Westerbork. And on September 5, 1944, the *Dolle Dinsdag*,[28] when the Dutch believed they had been liberated, the Nazis transported my mother to Auschwitz.

I can remember a little about the period after we ended up in the Hollandsche Schouwburg for the first time. I don't know if we were betrayed and picked up, or how we were taken to the Schouwburg. One memory that has stayed with me is the dim light in the theater and the red chairs we sat on while we waited to find out what would happen to us. They took my brother and me, along with the other children, to the kindergarten across the street, where the staff helped us to escape through the gardens, and we were taken back to my Aunt Lena's house on Nieuwe Herengracht.

Aunt Lena was married to Eli Talhuizen, an orthodox Jewish man who had a grocery store on Waterlooplein. He'd heard that children in orphanages were not going to be deported, because they'd already been punished enough. Those kinds of rumors were often started by the Germans themselves. So my uncle

---

28. *Dolle Dinsdag* (Dutch: Mad Tuesday): Tuesday September 5, 1944. The Belgian cities of Antwerp and Brussels had been liberated two days before, and the Dutch thought they would soon be liberated as well. Everyone was mad with happiness. However, it was not until May 5, 1945, that the Netherlands was finally liberated.

managed to get us sent to the boys' orphanage. I have no idea how long we were in there. What I remember about the orphanage is the window in the door and the steep staircase.

But, of course, on March 6, 1943, on **Shabbat**,[29] the Germans went ahead and emptied the orphanage anyway, and we ended up in the Hollandsche Schouwburg for the second time. The following Tuesday we were taken to the Oostelijk Havengebied station, where many of the trains to Westerbork departed from.

As soon as we were on the train, while it was still waiting to leave, my brother and I started looking for escape routes. We had already looked in the lavatory — maybe that was an option. Then suddenly we heard someone shouting, *"Waar zijn de Jasjes? Waar zijn de Jasjes?"* Where are the Jasjes? Our mother's surname was Jas, which is the Dutch word for coat, and a *jasje* is a little coat. So anyone else would have thought that the man was looking for jackets, but my brother knew straightaway that he meant us. A truck was driving alongside the train and the driver kept calling out, "Where are the Jasjes?" We squeezed through to an exit and, as the truck passed in front of the door, we jumped in.

The truck belonged to Mr. Grootkerk, our aunt Lena's neighbor. His transport company delivered supplies for the trains. Grootkerk had heard from Lena that we were on the train. As he was making his delivery, he'd gone looking for the Jasjes, the jackets — for my brother and me. Grootkerk kept the goods for the train on the passenger seat in his cab. There was a large space beneath the dashboard, where we had to hide beneath a sheet of

---

29. **Shabbat**: the Jewish day of rest. Shabbat runs from a few minutes before sunset on Friday until the appearance of three stars in the sky on Saturday evening and is intended as a day of rest to honor God and the creation of the heavens and the earth.

brown tarpaulin. If we squatted down, we fit just fine. In total, Grootkerk helped sixteen children escape from the trains that way. The guards never noticed a thing. They knew Grootkerk, and they just waved him on when he left the site.

Soon after our escape, some students from **Piet Meerburg's group**[30] took us to Utrecht. We stayed in the basement of a house at first, where it was so dark that we had to have the lights on even in the daytime. There was a small window near the ceiling, and if we looked out we could see legs walking past — not shoes, not upper bodies, just legs. And that's what we looked at all day long.

After that we ended up with some elderly people who thought we were children from Rotterdam, which had been bombed flat. The front room of the house had a view of the street. On the birthday of Mussert, the leader of the NSB, there was an NSB flag hanging outside the old folks' home across the street. My brother said, "Someone ought to shoot that flag to ribbons."

"Why's that?" they said. "Don't you think it's a nice flag?"

A few days later, they asked my brother to fetch something from the dresser. My brother, who could already read, spotted a copy of *Volk en Vaderland* in the drawer, the weekly newspaper for NSB members.

A man used to come by occasionally to check up on us. He was from the resistance, but only we knew that. My brother told him about the flag and the magazine. The elderly couple were quiet people and maybe they only supported the NSB as a political

30. **Piet Meerburg's group**: a resistance group that arranged safe houses for Jewish children.

party, but the resistance still thought the situation was too risky. They split us up after that. I went to stay with the Protestant Borg family, who made me kneel and pray on the cold linoleum beside my bed every night.

They kept a braid of their dead daughter's hair by my bedside, which I thought was kind of nasty. One of the sons was mentally handicapped. He adored me. I think they were probably aware that the little boy they had taken in was Jewish.

The people at my next address definitely knew I was Jewish. They built a peat bin[31] in the attic for me to hide in. Whenever the bell rang, they chased me upstairs, and someone would lift me into the peat bin. It was a cozy fit. As soon as I was sitting down, the lid went on. Then they would lay some blocks of peat on top. There were also peat blocks piled up around the walls of the bin, so that it looked as though they had a large supply of peat. That address was just a temporary hiding place as well. Even with my peat bin to hide in, it was still too dangerous.

Then some resistance members took me on a steam train to Bilthoven. It was a warm day when I arrived, sometime in August 1943. I didn't need to hide when I got there. My new family didn't even mention a hiding place. They let me have the run of the garden of their big house. The family had three children, two boys and a girl who was a little younger than me. The children accepted me immediately and let me play on their bikes and their Autoped.[32] Finally I was with an affectionate family and I had friends to play with.

---

31. peat bin: a place where people kept chunks of peat, pieces of decayed vegetation that are dried and can be burned as fuel.
32. Autoped: an early kind of motor scooter.

Maurice (on the far right) celebrating his birthday in Bilthoven, 1944

My new foster mother, Zus Boerma-Derksen, was part of a resistance group that had carried out various attacks on the railroad line used by the trains to Westerbork. When a traitor was found in the group, they asked her to shoot the man dead. She did as she was told. Then she made a run for it, but she was arrested and sent to prison. She was released later because witnesses had described a woman in her early twenties and she was thirty-four at the time. She was small and slim, so she looked younger.

A high-ranking German officer lived in the house opposite ours. He used to hold big parties there, and we'd watch the men in open-top cars going up the driveway. We were actually in the lion's den, but it never caused us any problems.

There were lots of people in hiding in Bilthoven. The local resistance had destroyed the municipal register, which listed everyone who lived in Bilthoven, to make it possible for people to take on new names. Now that the register was gone, no one knew who lived where, so all of the residents had to report for a new register. This was a wonderful opportunity for people like me to change our names and become regular citizens of Bilthoven. I became Ries Boerma, and I was part of the family.

The Boermas welcomed me into their family. We all used to go on day trips sometimes. One time we went on the train to Woerden. I can still remember changing trains at Utrecht Station, where trains left for destinations all over the Netherlands.

On liberation day, my foster brother and I stood and watched as the Canadians drove into Bilthoven. The soldiers put up their tents in the gardens of the big houses. We thought it was wonderful, and we wandered all over the place, enjoying the chaos that reigned in those first few days after liberation. There were all kinds of ammunition piled up on Rembrandtlaan, whole cases full. I went along and picked out some bullets for my foster mother. I stuffed handfuls of them into my pockets. And we found some signal flares that belonged to the Canadians. My elder foster brother was technically minded. He cobbled together a flare gun and we used a hammer to set them off. They made a beautiful fireworks display.

My mother survived Auschwitz. The Germans transferred her to the labor camp at Liebau, where she worked in a factory that made tank tracks. That was her salvation. The chance of survival was far greater there than in Auschwitz. She was liberated by the Russians.

One day, my mother's brother came to fetch me. It was peach season, and my uncle bought four peaches for my brother and me. They cost ten guilders, which was a lot of money back then. When I saw my mother, I just said, "Hello, ma'am." She was really sad that I didn't recognize her right away. I felt relieved when my uncle took me back to Bilthoven at the end of the day.

At first we still hoped that my father was alive. My mother even went to Staphorst to see if she could find out anything about the time when my father had worked in the forest there. She also went to Westerbork. His name was on the deportation lists. We later found out that my father had been murdered on February 28, 1943, in Auschwitz. That means they weren't certain of the exact date. If they didn't know the date when someone was murdered, they used to put the last day of the month on the death certificate. I only have a very vague memory of my father from before the war.

The three of us went to Amsterdam. We had to go on a boat, because the trains weren't running yet. Soon after liberation, my mother asked if I'd ever been anywhere on the train during the war. I told her about my trip to Woerden. "That was the day," said my mother, "when I was taken away on the train. We were lining up to get on the train at Centraal Station in Utrecht, and suddenly I spotted you. It was awful to see you just walking along like that. I wanted to call out to you, but of course I kept my mouth shut, or you would have been arrested as well."

We had nothing left after the war. I had to wear what we called *kleppers*, a kind of wooden sandal. Then my uncle took us to a cobbler in the east of Amsterdam, who made us each a pair of shoes — the only handmade shoes I've ever had. The government gave our mother coupons to buy things. But there was nothing to buy. If she heard in the morning that a particular item was going to be on sale that day, she would line up to see if she could get some. She often didn't return until four in the afternoon.

My mother was broken by the war. Having to struggle to survive for years had made her selfish. She was only really capable of loving herself. And she was jealous of my foster mother, whom I saw more as my real mother, because she was so kind to me. My mother tried to break the bond between my foster mother and me.

In 1981, when my foster mother was seventy, we had a big celebration. She rented vacation homes for all of the children and grandchildren. We traveled by public transportation and were the last to get there. As we entered the room where the party was being held, my foster mother smiled and said, "Good. Now I have all of my children and grandchildren together in one place."

Sieny Kattenburg, c. 1940

UNCLE HENK'S CHILDREN

SIENY KATTENBURG

Born in Amsterdam, March 19, 1924

When Jewish students were made to leave school at the beginning of 1941, a friend of mine said, "Sieny, we'll go to work. Let's apply to the kindergarten on Plantage Middenlaan. They need staff there." The kindergarten took care of both Jewish and non-Jewish children. The staff was also "mixed."

The director, Mrs. Henriëtte Henriquez Pimentel, took us both on and we started our training. In June 1942, the raids began. More and more Jews were being picked up on the street and taken from their houses at night. Sometimes they were transported directly to a concentration camp, but usually they were temporarily held in the Hollandsche Schouwburg. There was not much space in the theater, and the Germans found the children far too noisy and troublesome, so the kindergarten where I worked was designated as the reception center for the children. All of the non-Jewish members of the staff were fired, on the orders of the Germans, and no non-Jewish children were allowed in the kindergarten. From then on, we had to look after newborns, toddlers, and older children night and day, even though we had no beds, mattresses, playpens, or baby things. The Jewish Council took care of that, and the food as well. The director nominated three girls to be responsible for the three age groups. I was given the little ones, from newborns to four-year-olds.

I had to visit the Hollandsche Schouwburg every day, which was never designed to hold so many people. There were people sitting on the floor and on the old theater seats, and there was straw on the floor for them to lie on at night. The building stank. There were only a few bathrooms in the whole place. In the first few weeks after the Germans had taken charge of the kindergarten, the mothers were still allowed to cross the street to feed

Sieny with a toddler in the kindergarten, 1942

their babies. But the Germans stopped that later, and we took the children to their mothers in the Schouwburg.

Everyone wanted to get out of the Schouwburg. Whenever I took a child back to the kindergarten, their parents would stop me. "Can I come with you too?" "Please take my son away from here!" One time a boy was crossing the street with me and he made a run for it. The Germans chased after him, with their rifles drawn. And I ran after him too. If I hadn't grabbed hold of him, they would have started shooting.

At the entrance to the Schouwburg, the Jewish Council had made a reception area where people were registered when they entered the building. All of the names and addresses were written on lists, so that the Germans would know exactly who was there. Some of the council staff tried to keep as many children off these lists as possible, so that they could be smuggled out again later. It worked like this: When a family turned up with three children, they would write, for example, "Cohen family, two children." One of those three children was now "illegally" in the Hollandsche Schouwburg. Although there were only two children on the list, we would take three across the street the next day. So now there was one child in the kindergarten who was not on any list. And as long as they were not on a list, the Germans wouldn't miss them.

The Germans sometimes used to come and inspect the kindergarten. One time a large gang of them came stomping up the steps in their jackboots. When they were about to march into the dormitory, I stood in their way and said, "Get out of here, how dare you wake up little children!" And they left, as meek as lambs.

There were often several transports a week to Westerbork. The Germans knew exactly who was to be deported each time. It was all carefully controlled. But the director of the Schouwburg, Walter Süskind, who was a German Jew, had succeeded in winning the trust of the Germans, and he always told our boss who would be leaving that night. I would go over to the Schouwburg and take the parents to one side. "I'd like a quick word," I used to say. "What I'm telling you is strictly confidential. You're on the list for Westerbork. They'll be taking you at ten o'clock tonight. But one of your children isn't registered. Do you want us to bring the child this evening or would you prefer to leave it with us?"

The parents nearly always started to panic. "What should we do?"

"You have until four this afternoon to decide," I would say. "I'll come back then."

At four o'clock I would go talk to them again. "What did you decide?"

Most of them wanted to keep their children with them. "We're young and strong," they used to say. "We can take care of our children ourselves." If they decided to leave the child behind, they would say, "Make sure he ends up somewhere he can have a good life, with kind people."

"We will," I used to say. "We'll make sure everything's all right until you come back." And that's what I believed.

We did something similar with babies that were registered, but that was more difficult. When we heard that the family was to be deported that evening, one of us would go to the parents and ask the same question: "Do you want to take your baby or leave it with us?" And again I would go back at four o'clock. If the parents wanted to take the baby, we would wake the child at nine in the evening, give it a bottle and take it to Mom and Dad. If the parents decided to leave the baby with us, I'd say, "I'll come at half past nine and instead of your baby I'll bring you a doll, wrapped in a blanket. If anyone wants to take a look at it, you have to say it's sleeping." In a daze, the parents would nod and then, later that evening, they'd climb into the truck with a doll in their arms.

So then the children were in hiding with us in the kindergarten. Sometimes we would put the babies into bags and carry them to people from the resistance, who found places for them to hide. We used to give them a spoonful of wine so that they would sleep. Older children escaped via the teacher-training college, which had a backyard adjoining the kindergarten's.

The director of the teacher-training college was in on the operation. He'd cleared out a classroom inside the college and put in a number of beds where the children could sleep. The resistance would then come to collect the children from him. The resistance members went into the teacher-training college through the front door with everyone else. Students were going in and out of the building all day long, so no one paid any attention. They just had to pick the right moment to walk back out with a child. Strangely, none of the students ever noticed that anything unusual was going on.

Other children "disappeared" when we took them out for walks. We would go out with a group of children to a nearby street, Plantage Parklaan, where someone would be waiting to take one of the children into hiding. When we were almost there, I'd take the child aside, point at the man who was waiting, and say, "That man over there is your uncle, and he's going to take you to a farm." I just used to make it up. Then we'd walk back, and I'd return to the kindergarten with one child fewer.

It usually went smoothly, as the Germans rarely checked how many children had left and how many returned. But we always had a lookout, and when there was a German at the door who might have been counting, someone used to give me a sign. I'd signal back with my hand: one child gone, or two. The lookout would race upstairs, and some children would come tearing back down. They'd already be jumping up and down on the doorstep before the German could start counting properly. All told, at least five hundred children went into hiding via the kindergarten.

As I was walking down the steps with a group of children one day, a courier entered the building. He was wearing a star and an armband with a number from the Jewish Council, which showed that he was temporarily exempt from deportation. That armband also functioned as a permit to be out on the streets after the **curfew**.[33] We saw each other only briefly that time, as I was taking the children to their parents across the street. In the weeks after that, I saw the man more often. His name was Harry. There was a spark between us, and we fell in love. Harry tried to cycle by the kindergarten as often as possible, and he spent all of his free time with us. He also helped to smuggle children out sometimes, and he played games with them to keep them calm.

We got married on June 28, 1943, in our old rags because we'd taken our good clothes somewhere else in case we decided to

---

33. **curfew:** the time in the evening by which everyone had to be off the streets.

go into hiding. But I didn't want to do that yet. I didn't want to abandon the children.

On July 26, 1943, when Harry had been living with me up in the attic of the kindergarten for just a few weeks, the Germans emptied the place for the first time. Suddenly there was a bunch of trucks at the door, with Dutch police and Germans, who had a list of the names of the staff members, including our boss, Mrs. Pimentel. I was able to snatch a piece of cake and bread from the table before we were taken to Muiderpoort station, from where the train to Westerbork would leave.

We were there until midnight, and no one knew what was going to happen. Suddenly there was an announcement that *"Frau Cohen vom Kinderhaus"* (Mrs. Cohen from the children's home) should make herself known. Surrounded by SS men, I had to climb into a truck. Until that night I hadn't been scared, but then, there, at the station, I was terrified. What was going to happen to me? We stopped at Frederiksplein, where they made me get into another vehicle. At one in the morning, we raced across a completely deserted Amsterdam. They dropped me off at the kindergarten across from the Schouwburg: *"Und jetzt sind Sie Direktorin,"* they said. "And now you're the director." It was insane. I was far too young to be in charge. Fortunately a much older colleague of mine also came back the next day and she took over the management instead.

Later I heard from Harry, who had been away when the kindergarten was emptied, that he had gone to look for me. He'd said, "Either I'm getting her out of there or you can transport both of us together." But he couldn't find me because I was already on my way back to the kindergarten. Luckily he went back to the kindergarten too, where we found each other again.

• • •

We continued our work at the kindergarten until the morning of September 29, the day before Rosh Hashanah, the Jewish New Year. At that point, the kindergarten was almost empty. There were hardly any Jews left in Amsterdam and we knew it was only a matter of time before we would be deported ourselves. So we decided to go into hiding. Harry and I left in the early hours. On foot. It turned out that we had left just in time. The Nazis emptied the kindergarten for the last time that day. They dissolved the Jewish Council and sent all of the staff members to Westerbork.

We'd only just set out when someone came cycling past. We saw him look back over his shoulder. It was before eight and there wasn't a soul around. I wasn't even allowed to be out on the street before eight. Harry had his exemption, so he was all right. We walked on, but suddenly the man was standing there in front of us. He was a Dutchman who worked for the *Sicherheitsdienst*, the German intelligence agency. He was dressed in civilian clothes, not a uniform. The man glared at us and asked where we were going.

"Just out for a stroll," said Harry. "We have to get to work soon."

"Identity cards."

Harry handed him our own old ID cards.

He studied them carefully and then returned them. "Make sure you're at work in ten minutes."

As soon as he had disappeared from sight, we walked on to our first safe house. We went the rest of the way in silence, terrified that we would be stopped again.

When we got to the house, we cut the stars from our clothes. Then we rang the doorbell and the door opened. Without our stars, we headed upstairs, to the De Swaan family.

That same day, Mrs. De Swaan's gardener, Hannes Boogaard, came to fetch me. We traveled to the Boogaards' family farm in Nieuw-Vennep, about twenty miles south of Amsterdam, first on the tram, and then on the bus. The family took in so many Jews that the bus driver even used to announce, "Jews for Boogaard, this is your stop!" It was a bad business. Many of the Jews who were hiding on the farm were betrayed.

Boogaard's place was teeming with people. There were around sixty Jews staying there. Harry had also arrived there by then, and that evening Hannes took us on his bike to a houseboat on the Lisse canal. I saw cows and grass and meadows for the first time in ages. Up on that dike, on the bicycle, I felt free. It was wonderful. Briefly, we were safe from the worry that the Germans might pick us up at any moment.

We saw the houseboat in the distance. There was a man standing in the doorway. It was Kees van Tol. "You're bringing me more Jews?" he asked Hannes when we stepped off the bike. "I can't take them. We've just had a raid."

"You have to take them," said Hannes. "I can't take them back with me either."

There were huge bunches of gladiolus in the living-room window. I asked if they'd had a party.

"No," said Van Tol. "It's to make sure no one can peer inside."

There was no clean water, no light, no gas. We slept on a wooden bench that night. Just before we went to bed, he brought us his own sheet, and he also gave us a chamber pot.

As there had recently been a raid and the Germans nearly always returned to the same address one more time, he told us that we'd have to go out through the window and into the canal if his dog started yapping. He said the dog never barked, but no sooner had he left than the dog started barking away. So we hid in the water, clinging to the edge of the boat. False alarm. The next morning, Van Tol took the dirty chamber pot, rinsed it in the canal, rowed to the opposite bank, fetched some water from the pump, rowed back, and said, "Here's some drinking water for you."

We couldn't stay on the houseboat at night, as the risk of another German raid was too great. Van Tol told us about an island, not far away, where some of the locals had hidden a boat in a shed so that it wouldn't be confiscated by the Germans. "I'll lend you my rowboat," Van Tol said, "and you can spend the night over there, on the boat. But you'll have to go there in the dark and come back in the dark."

As we were rowing there, we heard splashing in the water. "They've found us," said Harry. But nothing else happened. We reached the island, opened up the shed and climbed into the boat. No sooner were we on the boat than we heard more splashing, and then more. Soon it was coming from every direction: *splash, splash, splash*. Rats! The whole place was crawling with them. We rowed over there every night for two weeks. We didn't sleep, and after that first night we didn't take any food with us, because that's what had attracted the creatures. We sat huddled on the boat, holding hands, terrified that the rats would walk on us again.

Two weeks later, a young man from the resistance brought some ration cards to Van Tol's. We started talking. He told us about his parents, his brothers and sisters, and about the Jewish people they were sheltering: a few children and an older man. He never should have told us, but his story was a stroke of good luck for us. Harry had heard that his father was hiding in a place with some young people.

"What's the older man's name?" asked Harry.

"Uncle Henk," said the man.

Harry's father's name was Salli, but everyone took on different names when they went into hiding, so Harry took out the photograph of his father that he carried with him and asked, "Is this him by any chance?"

"Yes," he said. "That's Uncle Henk."

And that's how we found out that Harry's father was hiding in a house nearby.

"I'll go home," said the young man, "and see what I can do."

So he went home. "You'll never guess who I just met," he told his mother, Mrs. Breyer. "Uncle Henk's children. They're in a bad position, no water, nowhere to sleep." When Harry's father heard that, he started crying.

"Don't cry," said Mrs. Breyer. "We'll go fetch your children tomorrow."

The next evening, that young man, Piet Breyer, and his brother came to get us.

It was like going from hell into heaven. The Breyer family had a small house on the dike, about four yards by six. It was lovely and cozy inside. There were already sixteen people there: eight Jewish people in hiding and eight family members, including a son who was hiding in his own house to avoid being sent to Germany as a forced laborer. Harry's father, whom we immediately started calling Uncle Henk, cried. Mrs. Breyer, whom we called Aunt Ant, was beaming. We all drank tea together. Everyone was in a festive mood: Uncle Henk's children had arrived!

The Breyer family's house, between the towns of Nieuw-Vennep and Haarlemmermeer.

Soon after we got there, Mr. Breyer, whom we called Uncle Sam, found a crack in a wall of the crawl space beneath the house. That crack was a sign from God, he said, telling him to make another space there, a secret one. The basement was only about thirty inches deep. They couldn't dig any deeper because the groundwater would have come in. The sons worked on it for weeks, digging during the day and scattering the soil over the fields at night. We made a wooden hatch for the hole in the wall and then knocked nails into it and tied string between them. That was so we could spread cement over the hatch and it would stay in place. The hatch had a handle on the inside so that the last person in could close it behind them. It looked exactly like the wall around it. The only light and air came in through the ventilation holes at the back of the house.

At first we only slept in there at night, until the Germans started doing random searches of the local houses. Then Aunt Ant decided that it would be a good idea to split us up: five upstairs and six under the ground one day, and the other way round the next day. We all ate upstairs though, until one day the Germans came to search the house when we were sitting at the table. As usual, Harry's father was at the head of the table and keeping look-out. We had finished eating and just as the oldest son picked up the Bible, Harry's father cried out, "*Sicherheitsdienst!* Quick, hide!"

Everyone flew to the basement. The plates, the pans — Aunt Ant threw them all into the sink. Then she positioned Gerrie, their disabled daughter, on top of the entrance to the crawl space. The Germans saw through that trick. They pushed Gerrie out of the way and one of the men came down into the basement. We could hear someone searching, and getting closer and closer to our hiding place. I expected the light to shine in my face at any moment. But the man didn't notice the hatch in the wall, and he went back upstairs. We were all so relieved, but I couldn't stop thinking about the huge pile of dishes that had been thrown into the sink. They didn't spot them either.

Angry that they hadn't found anything, they took the eldest son, who was called Sam, like his father, and dragged him outside. We could hear everything through the floor and we were terrified that Sam was going to be arrested or even shot.

"Where are the Jews?" they asked.

"Jews?" he said. "We've never met any Jews. I don't even know what Jews look like."

"There are Jews here. We're certain of it. That's what everyone's saying."

"So you believe gossip, do you?"

"Yes," they said. "There's usually some truth in it."

"Well, it's up to you what you do, but I've never seen a Jew in my life."

Sam wasn't taken away, and he wasn't shot. After a while, he came back inside and the Germans left. His parents and his brothers and sisters didn't bat an eyelid.

After that search, we must have spent an entire year in the ground. We went upstairs only to stand upright for a short while and have a wash. We had to lie on straw, which was only changed when the pigs had clean straw too. In all those months, it happened once or twice.

After December 1944, there were no more searches of the house. That was probably because after the seventh visit, Uncle Sam had asked the Dutch police where he should direct his complaint. "This is the seventh time you've been here," he said. "You people have come from Amsterdam, then from Haarlem, and then from Leiden. Shouldn't it be clear by now that you have no business here? I want to lodge a complaint because these visits are a real nuisance." Then Aunt Ant wrote to the mayor to say she didn't want to be disturbed again, because it should be obvious by now that they weren't hiding any Jews.

We were never really starving. We even used to have a slice of cheese with our bread. We'd place the cheese on the first piece of bread and slide it onto the second when we started to eat and we didn't eat the slice of "sliding cheese" until we got to the last piece of bread. When people came begging at the door during the Hunger Winter, Aunt Ant called us all together and said, "How about we all eat one less piece of bread each?" she asked. "Then we'll have some to give away." And so that's what we all did, including her sons, who worked on the land all day long.

On the morning of May 5, Aunt Ant called down to us in the basement: "Come out! The Germans have surrendered. You can go outside!" We crawled out of the basement, which wasn't easy, because we all had such stiff knees. Ten minutes later, we heard shouting:

"Get back inside! They're still fighting out there."

"I'm not going back inside," said Harry. "If the Germans come now, I'll join in with the fighting." But that didn't happen.

"So, the war's over now," said Aunt Ant. "But would you mind staying here until next Sunday? I'd like us all to go to church together."

The walk to church wasn't easy, because our legs were out of the habit of walking. The church was packed on that first Sunday after the end of the war. We were the last ones to enter the church: the Breyer family and the eleven people who had hidden with them. The people in the congregation couldn't believe their eyes. There were seats reserved for us in the front pew and the minister dedicated his entire sermon to Aunt Ant and Uncle Sam. For Aunt Ant, it was an unforgettable moment of glory.

I've often said that the time after the war was ten times worse than the war itself. During the war we were living in a kind of daze: All we thought about was liberation, and all we hoped was that we would make it to the end. There was no chance for any other thoughts.

In the weeks and months after liberation, it felt as if we were waking up and experiencing the real tragedy. Nearly all of our relatives were dead. Other people were living in our house. For a while we had to live in the storeroom at my father's warehouse. But still I walked to Centraal Station every day to see if my father was on the list of people who were coming back. Someone said they'd seen him somewhere in Poland. But it was no good. His name appeared on the list three times — and every time it turned out to be a mistake.

The Breyer family with all the people who were hiding in their house (except for Harry's father), taken after the liberation, 1945. Harry is in the back row, second from the left. Sieny is in the middle row, third from left.

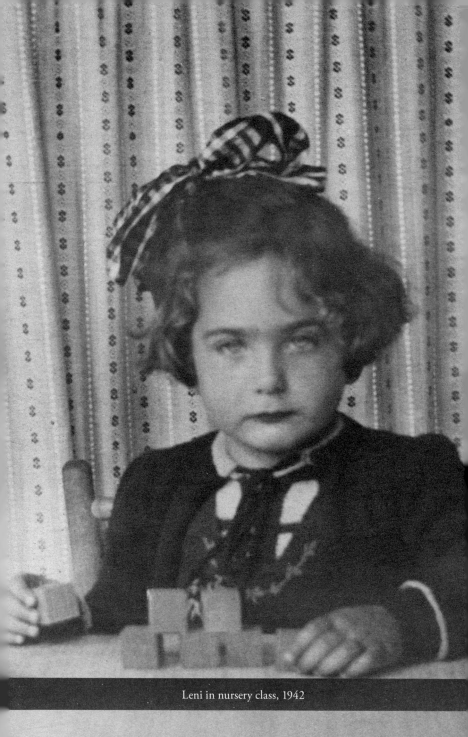
Leni in nursery class, 1942

AUNT NELLY

LENI DE VRIES
Born in Neede, eastern Netherlands, February 20, 1938

I can still remember having my tonsils taken out. It was 1941 and I was three years old.

They gave me a white basin to hold, with two handles and a blue rim. I was wearing a brown rubber apron, which the nurses had pulled over my head. I placed the white basin on the apron. Then the doctor came in and he started cutting away with a kind of salad fork and spoon. I don't remember the rest of the operation, or even the pain. What I do remember is having to spend the night in the hospital and sleeping in a crib with wooden bars. I needed to go to the bathroom during the night. They put me on a bedpan, one of those old-fashioned chamber pots. It was awful. My parents weren't allowed to come in to see me because of the risk of infection. Someone gave me a doll. I thought it was a nurse who gave it to me, but I later found out that it was from my grandmother. That's my first memory. I was truly alone, and there was no one to comfort me.

Before the war, my father had a kosher[34] butcher's shop. Like the other Jewish butchers in the village, he only sold beef, while the three other butchers in Neede sold pork. After the war, that all changed. The other butchers started selling beef, so my father had to sell pork too. My mother once told me later that she tried to keep Shabbat, but we often had to wait so long for my father that we fell asleep over our food.

For me, being Jewish was all about the feeling of security that my grandmother gave me. She was a large woman, and she used to wear a dress with a big silver brooch pinned to it. I loved sitting on her lap. That dress was very special to me. It was such an

---

34. kosher: food and drink that conforms to Jewish dietary laws.

unusual shade of brown, a sort of dark bronze color, and it seemed to radiate warmth. I've never seen that kind of brown since.

When we went into hiding, my grandparents didn't want to go with us. "We're not leaving Neede," they said. "We've lived here all our lives." They were taken from the house soon after that and murdered in Sobibor on May 14, 1943.

I don't actually remember anything about the war until the point I went into hiding, in early September 1942. I was four and a half years old. My younger twin sisters, my six-week-old brother, and my parents went into hiding at the same time — all of us in different places.

On August 25, 1942, my father was told to report to a labor camp. He was planning to go, because he said that work never killed anyone. The authorities let him off for a few weeks because of the birth of his son. Someone from the resistance advised him to go into hiding. They had addresses of safe houses for us. My parents followed the advice.

The hairdresser in Neede, Mr. Grunnekemeijer, came to fetch me. He took me to Enschede in a black car.

"Did you cry when I left?" I asked my mother later.

"No," she told me. "That would only have made it more difficult for you."

Mr. Grunnekemeijer stopped the car and said, "You have to get out here." We were on a bridge. I thought it was strange that there was no water under the bridge, just trains passing through. "Walk down that way," he said, pointing. "Then you'll come to a house. That's where you need to go."

Leni with her mother at the beginning of 1942

I walked down and rang the bell. A very kind man opened the door. He took me to the kitchen and gave me something to drink. I remember the red-and-white curtains at the windows. It was just like Hansel and Gretel's house.

Later I found out that the kind man was Reverend Overduin. Reverend Overduin was in the resistance and all throughout the war he looked for places where Jews could go into hiding.

After a while, a woman came to the house. I immediately took a dislike to her, but I had to go with her. She had five children, and I was the sixth child in the house. I was a dark-haired little girl, and my eyebrows met in the middle. They must have thought it made me look too Jewish, because almost as soon as I got there, they shaved the space between my eyebrows, without explaining anything to me. I felt as though I'd lost my identity somehow.

On Saturdays, Aunt Nelly used to give us a good wash. That's what I called her: Aunt Nelly. I never called her Mother or Mommy. She washed us in the kitchen. They didn't have a shower. She made me stand on a yellow kitchen chair. I still detest yellow chairs even now. Before she started scrubbing me, she slapped me so many times that I was black and blue until the following Saturday.

I've never been a fast eater. Aunt Nelly used to take my plate away halfway through the meal, saying that I obviously didn't like the food. Then she would give it to her son, who was ten years older than me. We got a cup of milk to drink with our food, but she used to top up my milk with tap water.

"Why do you always add water to my milk?" I asked her one day.

"I don't," she said.

"But I saw your hand going under the tap with my cup."

"No, you didn't."

Even after I'd caught her at it, she still kept topping up my milk with water. She didn't make any effort to hide it. I thought it was very odd that adults could fib like that.

One time, all of us children became sick, and Aunt Nelly put us all in one room. When we had almost recovered, we got rowdy and we started horsing around on the beds and broke one of the springs. I immediately got the blame, without Aunt Nelly even making an attempt to find out who'd been jumping on the beds. As punishment, she sent me into the hallway and made me stand on the granite floor in my bare feet. And keep on standing there. If I even thought about sitting down, she'd give me a good smack.

Aunt Nelly's husband, Jan, worked a lot and was hardly ever at home. But I think he must have sensed that I was missing out, because he sometimes used to sit me on his lap and give me a hug. I liked that. It felt like he was protecting me.

I didn't have an actual hiding place, but we once had some visitors who weren't allowed to know I was there. Aunt Nelly rolled me up in a piece of carpet and then leaned it up against the wall of the storage room. It was really cramped. I could barely move and my legs were really tired. Then I got cramps and I was terrified that I wouldn't be able to keep it up and that I might even fall over. It seemed to take forever before they came to unroll the carpet and I was free again.

In the family's dresser there were passport photos of my parents, which had been taken for their identity cards. I have no idea how they got there. Whenever I was having a really bad time, I used to sneak a peek into the dresser and hold the photographs for a moment.

In 1944, Aunt Nelly became pregnant again. I had to leave the house around the time of the sixth child's birth. They found a place for me with a doctor in the village of Enter. They were an elderly couple who also belonged to Reverend Overduin's congregation. It was like heaven: They didn't beat me, they didn't snatch my plate away, they didn't water down my milk, and they didn't make me stand on the ice-cold floor.

The war had also reached Enter, of course. I didn't know the word *raid*, but one day it became clear that I wasn't safe. The couple took me up three flights of stairs to a bedroom. Then they removed the bottom of the closet and I had to go back down another three flights of stairs to a room that was full of all kinds of girls' toys, which had belonged to their daughters. "You mustn't ask any questions," they said. "And you mustn't shout. We'll come fetch you when everything's safe again."

After sitting in that room for hours, I desperately needed to pee. But there was nothing that looked like a potty. So I found a yellow duster. I put the duster on the floor and I peed on it. The strange thing was that they weren't even angry when they came to get me. In fact, they even praised me for using the duster.

I once went with the man — I can't remember now what I used to call them — to pick nettles to make soup. We were both wearing gloves and he took me by the hand. I remember feeling calm and contented.

I also went to school in Enter. It was a religious school, but I don't remember much about it. I don't even know if I still had my own name. I do remember thinking it was crazy that things were just going on as usual: children walking to school, adults going to the movies or out dancing. Why should I be afraid when other people were just getting on with their lives?

Later, toward the end of the war, I had to go back to Aunt Nelly's house in Enschede. I was packed off like a parcel. The house was next to a park with a tennis court. One day, on the other side of the park fence, I saw a girl who was also on her own. I walked up to the fence, we talked for a while, and we played with those white berries that burst when you squeeze them.

When I saw my twin sisters again after the war, I suddenly remembered the girl from the park. Without knowing it, I had been playing with my little sister Mary. She was in hiding with "Aunt Bep" and "Uncle Bram," a young childless couple who often used to play tennis in the nearby park. I'd always seen my sisters together before the war, so I didn't recognize her when she was on her own.

After the liberation of Enschede, in April 1945, I wanted to go straight to my parents. That wasn't possible though, because they were in Apeldoorn, which wasn't liberated until some weeks later.

My parents went into hiding in a forest at first, in a henhouse. "We could cackle fine, but we weren't too good at laying eggs," my mother used to say. It became too dangerous in the forest, so they went in an ambulance to Apeldoorn, where they spent the rest of the war. The people who took in my parents treated them very badly. Whenever they ate meat, they used to throw my parents the bones. They were sheltering people for the money the resistance gave them.

Being back with my parents didn't feel at all strange. I could still remember exactly what our house looked like, where the spoon rack was in the kitchen, where my doll's baby carriage stood. I was the only one of the children who remembered our parents. My sisters are still jealous that I can remember so much about that period. When I got older, I was surprised by the large number of memories and mental images I have from when I was a little girl, particularly because I remember absolutely nothing about the next few years, from the age of seven to twelve.

Those first few months after the war were hard for my parents. They suddenly had four children in the house, three of whom were crying, "I want to go back to my mommy." "You're crazy," I used to say to them. "You're with your father and your mother." My little brother was six weeks old when he left and three when he came back. Sometimes my mother used to say, "The boy meant nothing to me." Later there were remarks such as "just like his dad" or "a dead ringer for his grandpa," but at first that little child was a stranger to her.

I found it hard to become attached to people after the war. During the war I'd often longed for my parents, but once I was back at home I realized that something was broken. My mother was no longer able to make me feel safe and loved. When I had my own children, I found it very difficult to cuddle them at first. I never really used to hug my friends and family either. But at a certain point, I just decided that I should get used to it, because I realized that people liked it. That brought back some of the feelings of warmth and security, but affection was something that I had to relearn.

Benjamin Kosses, 1942

AS LONG AS YOU
GET MARRIED

BENJAMIN KOSSES
Born in Oude Pekela, northern Netherlands, October 25, 1921

In the years before the war, I used to bike about nine miles to school every day with around thirty other children. There were three other Jewish children in the group and a few boys from NSB families. We ate our lunch at school. Our mothers used to wrap up our sandwiches in old newspapers. One day, one of the boys unwrapped his lunch from *Volk en Vaderland*, the NSB newspaper. He spread out the paper on the table and pointed at a cartoon of a rich Jew with a beard who was being deported. He looked at me and said, "That's what they should do to all of the Jews."

"If you start going on about Jews again," I said, "I'm going to beat the living daylights out of you." The others fired us up. I gave him a whack. He hit back. Then I picked up a meter ruler and I lashed out at him. He ducked, and it slipped out of my fingers and flew straight through an old map on the wall. Everyone fell silent. I walked right out of that room and headed for the house of Mr. Jonker, the school principal. He opened the door with a sour expression on his face. Jonker hated being disturbed at lunchtime. I told him what had happened. "Just go back to school," he said. "I'll be there soon."

That afternoon at half past three, there was still no sign of the principal. I started biking home with the whole group. About halfway there, a bunch of boys, friends of the one I'd been fighting with, jumped out from behind some trees and pulled me off my bike. I dished out as many blows as I could, but there was no way I could take on eight of them. Finally we all landed in the ditch. The boys and girls I biked to school with every day didn't lift a finger to help me, and they didn't even say anything either. I arrived home, covered in bruises, dirty and soaking wet, to find a bicycle propped up outside the house. Mr. Jonker was inside, talking to my parents. He was very much against the NSB, but felt that it was better not to speak out about it at school.

When I left school in 1936, I went to work for my father at first. He was a cattle dealer and butcher. He worked mainly with sheep and calves, and he often used to bring large herds over from Germany, just across the border. We slaughtered the animals ritually and kept to the Jewish traditions. My father used to get home by four every Friday evening, before Shabbat began and the work would stop.

After six months, my father said, "You should spend some time with someone else as an apprentice and see how things are done elsewhere." That's how I ended up with an aunt and uncle in Nieuwe Pekela who also had a slaughterhouse. I worked there until shortly after the war broke out. Then the Germans seized their business. That meant: cows gone, money confiscated, end of the slaughterhouse. My father also lost his cows. So a Christian colleague of my uncle's, Abraham Buzeman, offered me work. In 1941, it was still permitted for Jews to work with non-Jewish people.

When we were working in the slaughterhouse in Oude Pekela one day, a man called Koene came by. He was a butcher and he also belonged to an organization called Landwacht Nederland, which was a sort of special police force set up by the Germans and made up mainly of NSB members. With me standing right there, he said, "Bram, you need to get rid of that Jew assistant. He'll ruin your business."

"Koene, I'm the boss here, not you. Now clear off before I kick you out onto the street."

Koene left, but he came back later, in a black uniform and with two friends. They stood in the doorway and one of the men said, "Bram, you heard what Koene told you: You have to stop letting that Jew boy work in the slaughterhouse. Get someone else to do the work."

"I'll decide that for myself," said Buzeman.

There were six of us working that day, and there were three of them. But they were carrying shotguns. When one of them took his gun from his shoulder, we jumped on them and gave them hell. They stank of *jenever*.[35] They'd obviously helped themselves to a little Dutch courage before they came to see us.

After that I didn't go back to the slaughterhouse, but I continued to work for Buzeman at home, where we made sausages and other things. Koene must have heard about it, because he came to have another word with Buzeman. "Now you've got that Jew boy working at your own place. He's got to go. If you don't sort it out, I'll make sure you're carted off."

After Koene had left, I said, "I'm going. I can't stay here."

"You don't have to leave. I'll never let them have their way."

I left anyway. It was December 1941 and I went to work for a farmer in Nieuwe Pekela. They picked up Buzeman all the same and sent him to a concentration camp. He came back, but he caught a disease in the camp, which killed him soon after the war.

Six months later, my uncle came to see me. The local policeman had been to talk to him. "I've been told to arrest you and Bennie before Wednesday morning," he had said, "and take you to Winschoten and hand you over to the Germans at the station. I'm

---

35. *jenever*: Dutch gin.

not going to arrest you now, but if you're at home on Wednesday morning and you haven't taken the tram to Winschoten yourselves, I'll have to take the two of you in." We understood his warning.

"I'm not getting on that tram," I told my uncle.

"Me neither," he replied. "But where are you going to go?"

"I don't know."

"Let's go together. It'll be easier."

We left that same evening, at around ten o'clock. My uncle knew a man a few miles away who would help us. When we got there, we knocked on the doors, on the windows. No one came. I was so tired that I fell asleep in the garden, in the children's sandbox. My uncle sat waiting all night, worrying about the wife and three children he'd left behind.

In the morning, he hammered on the door again. This time someone answered. "Oh, you're here. Come on in." We spent the day in one of the bedrooms. At the end of the afternoon, the man came upstairs with a nervous look on his face. "My wife thinks you should leave, before the children get home. Our house is too small for us to hide people."

And that was our hiding place gone. It was a difficult time. I stayed at forty-two different addresses in three months. At first, I was still with my uncle, but after his wife and children had to go into hiding as well, that didn't work. It was November 1942 by then, a bitter winter, and it was freezing cold. I remember walking through the fields, with no idea where to go. I knew there was a cattle shed nearby and they're always warm. I found the shed, went inside, and lay down with the cows in the straw and fell asleep. The farmer found me in the morning, when he came to look after his cows. He knew who I was. "Fancy finding you in here!" he said. "How did you get in?"

"It wasn't difficult," I said. "The door was open."

"Yes, we don't lock that shed. You can stay in the house with us today, but make sure the farm workers don't see you. You'll have to leave when it gets dark." I understood that he didn't have the courage to take a Jew into his home, and at least I had a chance to sleep that day. I was able to warm up, and he gave me some food to take with me.

Then I went back to Nieuwe Pekela, to Hayo Kampion. He was a Jewish man, but he was married to a non-Jew, and so he was left alone. I knocked on the door, and Hayo answered. "Ah, come on in, son. Everyone's been saying you're in England."

"If only! No, I'm still here."

Kampion gave me some new clothes, which had belonged to his unmarried brothers who had already been taken away.

Another series of addresses followed. Finally I found myself with the Beuker family in Stadskanaal, a town just south of Nieuwe Pekela. They made me very welcome.

"You can milk and feed the cows, and work with the machines during the daytime." They gave me a decent place to sleep. I hadn't had it so good for ages.

A week later, the residential part of the farm buildings was **requisitioned**.[36] It wasn't so that Germans could live there but for NSB members who had come back from Germany. They'd hoped that the Germans would welcome them, but no one wanted them.

---

36. **requisitioned**: claimed by the government or the authorities for their use, particularly for military purposes.

"We'll board up a corner of the attic for you," said Beuker. "It may be for just another three weeks. By then the Germans will have lost the war."

I was up in that attic for fourteen days, in a wooden box that they'd built along the slope of the roof. It was dark up there, and I had a bucket to do my business in. One evening they came to fetch me. The NSB people were out for the evening, so I could have a wash and eat with the family. At dinner I said to them, "I can't stand it up there any longer. I want to leave."

"If you really want to go, I know an address for you. I'll go ask right now."

Fifteen minutes later, he returned, "Get your bike and your things. I'm taking you to the Drenth family. There's already a Jewish family there: a man, a woman, two children. You know them."

The Jewish family staying with the Drenths turned out to be another uncle of mine, who was there with his wife and two

The Drenth family's house

151

children. I knew them well. But it wasn't a warm family reunion. They immediately made it clear that I wasn't welcome, that I was an intruder in their world, a room of just over two hundred square feet, which they would now have to share with me, night and day. After only a few days, we had an argument about the lessons he was teaching his children. It was nonsense. He was teaching them half German, half Dutch. We were both really angry, but then his wife said, "Nico, just let him do it instead." So I started teaching the children math, Dutch, geography, and history, using school-books that one of the Drenths' daughters brought home from her school.

One evening, Mr. Beuker came to the house. He showed me a letter about the children of the uncle I'd been on the run with at first. They had to leave the place they were staying in Amsterdam. The money had run out. It was almost impossible for them to get hold of food and drink. "What should I do?" Beuker said.

"You'll have to ask Drenth," I said. "He'll know how to handle it."

Beuker went into the back room to discuss it with Drenth. I followed him, because I wanted to see what would happen. Father and Mother Drenth looked at each other and nodded. "You just bring them here."

Well, that really upset the uncle who was already there. He said there wasn't enough room for so many people, it was too dangerous, etcetera, etcetera. Until Mother Drenth looked at him and said, "These are your brother's children we're talking about." That shut him up.

Other people came to stay at the Drenths', including my sister, who had been hiding in henhouses with my parents, out in the countryside. But there was a raid and my parents were picked up. We never saw them again. My sister had been able to make a run for it just in time. She had a very good set of false papers that said she was a maid. She soon found it too cramped in that small space with us. She didn't look very Jewish, and so she was used to going wherever she pleased. She left us and went out to work for various families instead.

At one point, there were fourteen of us sharing those two hundred square feet. There were only two beds in the room, so at night we put sacks of straw and blankets on the floor. We got up early and kept to a strict schedule for washing and dressing, and we tidied the room before we went to bed so that it wouldn't become a complete chaos.

Every morning Drenth used to fetch two big buckets of water from the canal that ran past the house. The farm had no electricity, no running water, and no indoor toilet. We washed ourselves with water from the canal in a bedroom with a washbasin and an old-fashioned jug. During the daytime you couldn't go to the bathroom because you had to go through the whole house. We used a bucket instead. When the chairs were arranged around the table and everyone had washed, then we would each have a slice of bread for breakfast.

The Germans never raided the farm. They didn't become suspicious because Father Drenth had come up with a clever plan. He saw an advertisement in the newspaper one morning from a NSB office that was looking for a junior clerk.

"You're going to apply for that job tomorrow," he said to Lammie, his eldest daughter. Then he went to see an old friend of his, an NSB member with whom he still got along well. "Listen," he said, "could you explain to the people at the NSB office that my daughter has to have that job? She doesn't have any work, and we're not going to be able to manage at home for much longer."

She got the job, and the wages too. That office was where they planned the raids. And that's why we never had a raid at our house. Everyone in the village knew where Lammie worked. That made them suspect that the Drenths were Nazi sympathizers, and they would never have imagined that Jews were hiding at the farm. Their suspicions must have grown stronger after the director's wife, Mrs. Vuurboom, said to Lammie, "Your mother must often be alone at home when your father's out at work. I'd like to go over and have a cup of tea with her. It'd be nice to chat with someone for a while."

"Then let her come," said Mother Drenth to her daughter. "Invite her for the day after tomorrow."

So Mrs. Vuurboom came to visit. She was sitting no more than ten feet away from our hiding place, drinking tea. And she just kept on chattering away, even after Mother Drenth should have started preparing the food. The local farmers had seen that woman come into our house, so now everyone was sure to think that the Drenth family were Nazi sympathizers.

Everyone except for one neighbor. One sunny day she saw Mother Drenth hanging out the washing. She came over and said, "You mustn't do that. All of those things you're hanging up there don't belong to just your family. There's no need to tell me what's going on in your house, but you need to take that washing down, because if I can see it, other people can see it too."

Around that time, in the middle of 1943, I started getting to know Lammie better. She used to run errands for us sometimes. Once in a while she would take a list to Groningen to do shopping. We would give her some money, and she would set off with a suitcase. She brought all kinds of things back to the house.

From half past eight in the morning until midday, I kept the children occupied with schoolwork, but you had to entertain them somehow after that was finished. One day Father Drenth and I made a mouse cage out of glass and wood. But we didn't have any mice, so Lammie went to Groningen to get some. The mice went in the suitcase, together with all the other shopping she'd done that day, including some cake. The journey from

Bennie's parents with his sister Rebekka in the town of Voorthuizen, where they hid in a henhouse. They were betrayed in August 1943.

Stadskanaal to Groningen was a long one, as it was an old-fashioned slow train. And on the way back, the mice nibbled away inside the suitcase. There wasn't a crumb left of the cake!

On her trips to Groningen, Lammie's old school friends beat her up a few times, as they couldn't stand her going around with an NSB badge on her coat. When she got home, she was covered with bruises and her clothes were crumpled and torn. Her parents were too busy to worry too much about her. So we spent time together and we comforted each other. In that small space I shared, there were three married couples, two of them with children, but, like Lammie, I was on my own. I gave her a shoulder to cry on. When you're comforting someone, you touch, and sometimes things happen. We fell in love and then we had a new problem: Lammie was pregnant. Mother Drenth thought it was dreadful, absolutely terrible. Her father had a more practical attitude. "As long as you get married later, when this is all over, it's fine by me."

We could hardly buy any things for the baby. Everyone knew Lammie was working for the NSB, so shopkeepers refused to sell anything to her. Finally we found one company, where the Drenth family had never spent a penny before, that was prepared to sell things to them. They bought diapers, baby clothes, a crib, and all the necessary bits and pieces, for not too much money.

The birth, on December 10, happened in the living room. The doctor, Father and Mother Drenth, and I were all there with Lammie. When our daughter came into the world, she immediately started screaming so loudly that it woke up all the children in the house. Of course they knew what was going on; they'd noticed Lammie getting rounder. We fetched them out of bed that night to show them the baby. That set their minds at rest and all five of them went back to sleep.

After the war, we got married, just as Father Drenth wanted. Our eldest daughter is now sixty-five.

May 8, 1945, Bennie and Lammie's wedding day. Mr. and Mrs. Drenth (sitting on either side of Bennie and Lammie) with all of the Jews hiding in their home, and Mr. and Mrs. Brouwer, resistance workers who provided money and ration cards, back row, fourth and fifth from the right.

Michel with his sister Hansje, c. 1940

OLDER THAN MY FATHER

MICHEL GOLDSTEEN
Born in Meppel, northern Netherlands, May 5, 1933

My father had a wholesale business selling curtain fabrics. When he was traveling, I was sometimes allowed to share my mother's bed and do the shopping for her. It made me feel really close to her: I was the eldest son, the firstborn. My grandfather, my mother's father, lived with us. My grandmother had died in 1927 at a relatively young age. At that time it was fairly common to take in an elderly father to live with you. But that led to conflicts, because my grandfather and my mother were strict about following Jewish laws, while my father was not. Obviously everything in our house was kosher, but there were lots of other rules as well. For example, you weren't allowed to tear anything on Shabbat. So the mail remained unopened, and we had sheets of torn-off paper ready in the bathroom. We also had a Christian maid who turned on the lights in the house on Shabbat, because we weren't allowed to do that either.

When my father came home, he had to adapt to his father-in-law's religious views, which frequently annoyed him. He was far more relaxed about the rules. When he was out, he even ate pork, which is forbidden by Jewish dietary laws. On Saturdays I went with my father and grandfather to **shul**.[37] I was making good progress in my Hebrew lessons, partly because of the cookies in the shape of Hebrew letters that we got as a reward. When my Hebrew was good enough, I was allowed to read out a section of the **Talmud**[38] in the synagogue. I idolized my grandfather; he played a much larger role in my life than my father, who may not

---

37. **shul**: a Jewish place of worship where people come together to pray and learn. The word *shul* comes from Yiddish (the language of the Jews of eastern Europe) and is related to the German word *Schule* (school). *Shul* is another word for synagogue.
38. **Talmud**: a central book of Judaism, containing rabbis' commentaries on the Jewish bible (Torah) as well as Jewish law.

have been such a stickler for the rules of the faith but was still fairly strict about my upbringing. When my father came home from a business trip, he would ask me how I had behaved. And if I'd done something that was not allowed, then he would give me a scolding and sometimes even punish me.

Shortly before the war broke out, my father was thinking about emigrating to America. He already had the papers for the crossing with the Holland-America Line at home. But my grandfather wouldn't hear of it, and my mother was against the idea as well. After 1940, an administrator was assigned to my father's business, someone who took over the management of the company on behalf of the Germans. And although my father was a member of the Jewish Council and so he had a provisional exemption from deportation, he realized that we would not be safe for much longer.

When we had to start wearing the Star of David, in May 1942, my father decided to take some practical steps. He had my grandfather admitted to an old folks' home. We thought he would be safe there — no one expected that the Germans would also send older people to Germany. Everyone said they sent you to labor camps, and we couldn't imagine what use they might have for old people there. At the beginning of the war, I didn't think too hard about all the things that Jews were no longer allowed to do. As a little boy, I actually thought it was exciting to wear the Star of David. Sometimes my sister and I would turn our coats inside out so that we could buy candy at a store where it was illegal for Jews to shop.

At some point in September 1942, Guus Schraven came to visit us. He was a business associate of my father's. I don't know exactly what they discussed, but my father said, "You're going with Uncle Guus now, on the train. You have to go into hiding. Amsterdam has become too dangerous." There'd been a lot of talk about hiding in the previous weeks, but it still came as an unwelcome surprise. I knew that it meant we were going to be apart. Father and Mother told me that I absolutely must not mention my real name on the train or at my new address. "From now on, your name is Maurice Jansen." It was only temporary, and I knew that it was necessary.

I stayed with Uncle Guus in the north of Limburg for a few days and then he took me to a priest in Grubbenvorst. This priest found places to hide for lots of non-Jewish children from the west of the country, and later also Jewish children. He sent them to poor farmers who accepted money for taking in boarders. He found a place for me with the Theelens, a farming family with three children. He told them I was a boy from the city and that I'd come to the countryside to improve my health. That sounded entirely believable, as I was so skinny. The Theelens were rather doubtful at first, not because they didn't want to take in a little boy they didn't know, but because they thought I would feel out of place. They were just poor farmers, and I came from a well-off family. "How can we take care of a little boy like that?" they wondered.

I soon became used to life on the farm. I made friends with their son, Bert, who was a couple of years younger than me. The boys from the village were our playmates. We used to play soccer together, ride around in carts, fly kites, and hide among the tall asparagus plants. We also often used to wander over to an old ruin where we would wait in the dark to see the *witte wieven*,

The Theelen family's farm

patches of mist that swirled up as the evening cooled and looked like ghosts. We ran free, as though the war were far away.

The rest of my family had also gone into hiding by then. They were all in the province of Limburg, but in different places. One day, at about one o'clock, my father appeared on the doorstep, pushing a bike. The weather was fine, and he took me out for a ride on the back of his bike. I remember getting off the bike at one point and sitting with him on the roadside. He hugged me tight. I felt closer to him than I ever had been in Amsterdam. At the end of the afternoon he took me home. "I'll be back again soon," he said.

But, not long after that, someone gave away my father's location and he was arrested. They took him away, and we never heard from him again.

After my father's arrest, the priest thought he should inform the Theelen family about my Jewish background. The Germans might be able to use my father to find out the address of the place where I was hiding. "If you think it's too dangerous to keep Maurice with you," he said, "I'll find a place somewhere else for him."

"Maurice is here with us. We love him, and he's going to stay here," said Farmer Theelen. They knew now that they were looking after a child who was in mortal danger.

They made sure that I knew not to go shooting my mouth off to outsiders. That didn't apply so much to the neighbors; I think they knew what was going on. Maybe even the whole village suspected I was a Jewish boy in hiding. There were lots of other people hiding in Grubbenvorst too.

The Theelens warned me particularly about the local policeman, who was probably an accomplice of the village's NSB mayor. In all those years, he spoke to me only once. It was at a party. Suddenly he was standing beside me.

"You're not really Maurice Jansen, are you?"

"What do you mean?" I asked. "I'm Maurice Jansen, and I'm staying with the Theelens."

He never asked me any more questions after that. He probably didn't want to make himself unpopular in the village.

Even so, after my father's arrest, they still thought it would be safer if I went away for a while, to the place where my sister was in hiding. Farmer Theelen took me there on his bike. It was still light when we left. We rode along a railroad line for what seemed like forever. I had to sit on the back of his bike for more than twelve miles, and I was freezing, because it had become damp and cold as evening fell.

At about nine o'clock, we reached the house of the Simons family. Father and Mother Simons were sitting in the living room. Mr. Simons stood up, walked over to me, held my head in his hands, took a good look, and said, "You know, I can see it. You look just like your sister." My sister was already asleep, and they didn't wake her up. They gave me a room in the attic, where I spent the next few weeks, almost the entire night and day.

There were eight children in the family and only the eldest two knew that I was there. In the evening, after the other children had gone to bed, they came up to the attic with my sister. That was the high point of the day. I always looked forward to it.

After a few weeks, the Theelen family thought the coast was clear and I was allowed to go back to Grubbenvorst. In the evening again, on the bike again, along that railroad line again.

During the daytime I used to go out into the fields with Farmer Theelen and help him sow corn and dig up potatoes. On the farm, I swept the yard and fed the pig. When the pig had been fattened up, it was slaughtered. It made such a huge impression on me: the piercing screams of the animal before it was killed, the red jet of blood that spurted from the wound in its neck, which they used to make blood sausage, the sickening smell that rose up from the steaming entrails — entrails of an animal that had always been taboo to me, because Jews don't eat pork.

I couldn't go to school. It was too dangerous. So I used to walk to the edge of the village in the afternoon, where the Van den Bercken family lived. I had very good private lessons from Annie van den Bercken, who was a trained teacher, so that I wouldn't have any problems fitting in at school after the war. I was a quick student. When I'd finished my work for the day, I was allowed to go into her father's carpentry workshop, where I learned how to work with wood. The atmosphere at the Van den Berckens' house was different from the farm. It was more like being at home in Amsterdam: There was a bookcase, and they discussed issues that didn't come up at the farm. I felt at home there.

Grubbenvorst is close to the border so, from 1943 on, we saw lots of British bombers on their way to Germany. The Germans tried to shoot down their planes. The women and children would head for the air-raid shelters when that happened. Our shelter was at the neighbors' house. The men of the village usually stayed outside in a ditch during the raids so they could help the British if a plane came down.

On the night of June 24, 1943, planes were flying over again. We could hear it all from our shelter: the sound of the engine swelling and then the fading roar. Until suddenly there was a brief burst of furious gunfire, and an engine stopped, and everything went absolutely silent for a moment. Then we heard a high-pitched, shrieking sound, followed by such an enormous bang that all the sandbags barricading the basement windows came tumbling into the shelter. The light went out.

We tried to scramble outside. It didn't work. We started to panic, particularly the women. We children were really shocked too, of course, but we thought it was more exciting than scary. It turned out that part of the house above us had collapsed and there was debris blocking the door to the basement. We couldn't get out, so we were stuck in there until the men came back, cleared away the rubble, and opened the door. Then we saw the devastation in the village. Fortunately the Theelen family's farm was not seriously damaged.

Once every two months, my mother would come visit. It was a difficult journey on the bus, so she often used to stay the night. Those visits from my mother remain some of the most intense experiences of my entire life.

In the afternoon we would go for a walk and catch up on everything we'd missed out on while we'd been apart, and at night I was allowed to share her bed, the big bed in the attic. I thought it was wonderful. The next night, after she'd left, I'd sleep with her pillow, which still smelled of her. It was a sweet, lingering scent that I could smell for days.

After some time, my mother stopped visiting. "Why hasn't she been to see me?" I asked Father Theelen.

"She's sick," he told me. "She sent a message to say she'll be staying away for a while, but she'll come visit again soon." He kept giving me that answer for a few months, until I began to realize that there must be more to it.

I know someone gave her away, but I don't know who it was. What I do know is that my mother was sent to Westerbork. I have never found the scent of my mother's hair in any perfume since.

After my mother's arrest, I was sent to stay at yet another address for a while. This time it wasn't with my sister, but with the Van den Bercken family, where I used to go for my lessons. But now that I was living in their home, I was no longer allowed to spend time in the carpentry workshop. It was too dangerous. There were lots of raids in those months because the Germans were looking for men to do forced labor.

One of the carpenters made a partition in a big wardrobe on the first floor of their house, so there was a small space behind the clothes, where I had to sit in the daytime. I was allowed out in the evening, and at night I slept in their son Leo's room, who was away at school, studying for his exams.

I sat there on a stool, all day long. It was hell. It was impossible to lie down because the space was too small. Occasionally I was allowed to open the hatch for a short while, but all I could see was the clothes. I was really scared that I was going to be discovered.

After a few weeks I went back to the Theelen family's farm, where it was getting more and more crowded. During the last months of the war, the Germans made the Theelens take in a number of soldiers. Most of them were tired of Hitler and just wanted to go home. The Theelens were also sheltering two more Jews, a young married couple, Piet and Hennie.

Father Theelen and Piet hid in a space they'd dug out behind a wall in the barn in the courtyard. Hennie and I just walked around the house as usual. One of the soldiers was on our side. He told us that he was thinking of taking a bicycle and deserting, and he warned us about one of the other Germans in the house, who he said was still a committed Nazi. Having those German soldiers in the house had its advantages: When the German police were searching the area, they always left our farm alone.

On the night of November 25, 1944, the Germans evacuated the village. The day before, I'd heard at the Van den Berckens' that British soldiers were carrying out reconnaissance near

Grubbenvorst. Some people had even spoken to them. That night, German soldiers came and took us from the shelter. They ordered us to leave the village because they were going to blow it up. About an hour later, we were on the move, the priest with his cross leading the way, followed by the residents of Grubbenvorst. Taking only the most essential of our belongings, we headed toward the **front line**,[39] to Sevenum, which was about four and a half miles away.

It was a clear, cold night. The moon shone on the white ribbons that the British scouts had put up to guide the troops over a mine-free route the next day. A group of men from the village walked ahead, because we had to make sure the British knew that it was not Germans who were approaching but Dutch people from Grubbenvorst.

The first thing we saw — it must have been about four in the morning — was British artillery under big camouflage nets. Our liberators welcomed us. I can still remember thinking: I don't need to keep myself hidden anymore, I don't have to pretend to be someone else, I'm safe, the war's over for me. And it was true. In Sevenum we were put up with a family on a farm beside the railroad line.

We roamed around in the countryside during the daytime and looked for explosives along the railroad line, which we found lying around all over the place. Shells, cartridges, grenades — we found all kinds of things. We turned the war into a game. The British soldiers gave us chocolate and other good things to eat. One day, when we were playing beside the track, some British

---

39. **front line**: in a war zone, the area where the fighting is taking place.

jeeps that were driving along the railroad line got bombed. After the bombing, we went to take a look. We were really shocked by the sight of the dead and wounded British soldiers. There was heavy fighting in the area around Sevenum for months. It was actually far too dangerous to play there. We weren't allowed back to Grubbenvorst until the spring of 1945.

After the war I stayed on the Theelen family's farm for a while. For the first time, I went to a regular school. Finally I ended up in the same class as friends I'd been playing with on the street for years. We studied together to prepare ourselves for high school.

The newspapers printed lists of survivors. My parents, my grandfather, and many other relatives did not appear on the lists. My sister and I did. At first, we didn't believe that both of our parents had been murdered. We kept on hoping. Gradually we became used to the idea that they would never return.

I am now much older than my father was. I'm old enough to be my father's father. He was forty-three when he was taken away, and I'm now seventy-six. My eldest sons are already older than he ever was. When I stop to think about it, a strange feeling comes over me. Occasionally I try to imagine what my parents must have been through, on the train to Auschwitz, when they arrived at the camp. And after that. But then I get so angry that I think: This isn't good, I mustn't do this. That's why I've never visited Auschwitz or any other concentration camp. I'm afraid that the emotions would be overwhelming.

My feelings from back then are very distant. I can still see myself as a boy of six, seven, roaming around Amsterdam, ringing doorbells, getting into mischief. I can think about that boy, about his relationship with his father, with his mother, and with his grandfather. But I can't feel the emotions I had back then — it doesn't work. I just can't reach them anymore. Maybe I've automatically kept the past at a distance because I had to hide away for years and deny my background. Or maybe it's just that it's impossible to relive those feelings from the past, and so I have to make do with memories.

Lowina de Levie, 1937

JACQUES

LOWINA DE LEVIE
Born in Amsterdam, April 10, 1926

I was always a nervous child. I wasn't really teased or anything, but I never joined in with the other children in the school yard. I just used to stand and watch. My parents were always fighting, so I was too scared to take my friends home too.

We weren't poor but we weren't rich either. For lunch we had one slice of bread with some sort of topping, and the rest with plain margarine. My sister and I got a new dress twice a year. We thought that was plenty. I never minded that others in my class were better off. What I did mind was the bad atmosphere at home.

When war broke out, I was fourteen. I remember standing with my father and my eldest brother on the porch at about four or five in the morning. It was a beautiful night, a beautiful morning, but we could hear the drone of airplanes in the distance. I didn't understand what was really happening for a long time — not when the war started and not even when we went into hiding in 1943.

One day my eldest brother was picked up. Fortunately he came back home, but it gave my parents a terrible scare. That fear infected me, and it only became worse as the war went on, particularly after we were made to move to a small apartment in the Rivierenbuurt neighborhood of Amsterdam. The Germans housed the Jews in two or three areas of the city to make it easier for them to carry out raids. During that same period we were made to leave school. I didn't mind that so much. I'd just been held back a grade because I never did anything in school. All I did was draw. I used to draw pictures of happy families.

I had to walk half an hour every day to the Jewish School with my brother. I had a boyfriend at school, Jacques. We went skating together just once. He brought me home on his bike, and it was so windy that my eyes filled with tears. Oh God, I thought, why am I crying now, at this moment, when I'm so happy to be on the back of Jacques's bike?

Then we were no longer allowed on bikes, or into shops, and we had to wear a star — but none of that made much of an impression on me. The worst thing was the fear. I was particularly scared in bed at night. If I heard any noise at all, I thought it meant Jacques was going to be taken in a raid.

Then, one day, the Gestapo appeared in the doorway of our classroom at school. They read out his name: Jacques B. He stood up and said, "I'm young and I'm strong. I'll survive." He was wearing a good pair of walking boots and he had a backpack with him.

I knew at the start of the war that I was Jewish and that it was mainly Jews who were being taken away, but I still felt safe at that time. I was more scared that other people would be arrested. That made sense, as my father had secured a job for me with the Jewish Council. Anyone who managed to get a job with the Jewish Council was temporarily exempt from deportation.

The job my father got for me, as a housemaid, is what saved me. One day I was working at the house of an old lady who lived in the Rivierenbuurt district. Suddenly I heard the doorbell. And then the men from the Gestapo came storming up the stairs in their gray uniforms. My papers were in order, so I didn't have to go with them. The old woman did, though. They dragged her out of her bed and threw her into the back of an open truck. I have no idea if I slipped her anything to take along. Clothes or food. I can't even remember if I said anything to her.

At home we had a suitcase full of clothes ready for if we suddenly had to go into hiding. It wasn't meant for us to take if we were deported to the East — that was something we wanted to avoid at all costs. When I turned sixteen, I was no longer under my father's protection. As far as the Germans were concerned, I was now an adult and at any moment I could be called for deportation separately from my parents. At that point, we all went into hiding. Non-Jewish colleagues of my father's arranged the addresses for us. How they found them and how much it cost were subjects that no one mentioned, not even after the war. One thing was clear though: Money was necessary, and it was almost impossible for people without any money to go into hiding.

A woman who worked with my father took me to stay with a farmer just outside the village of Sint Jacobiparochie in Friesland. The farmer and his family had been living for years in a disused station on an old railroad line. They kept some pigs and a cow in a large room, which had probably once been the waiting room. I had a small room of my own up in the attic, where I could be alone.

I had no idea what living in hiding was going to be like. What I found most surprising was that there were places outside Amsterdam where a Jewish person could still have a nice life and people would treat you kindly.

The family had three children, a son who was a year younger than me, a daughter who was ten years younger, and a baby. I was really clumsy but, when the mother was ill, I still managed to look after the baby, cook the food, and run the household. They really needed me. I felt more at home there than anywhere else.

In Sint Jacobiparochie, where I did the shopping like any regular person, I was known as Loekie de Lange. The story we had to tell was that my sister and I had left Amsterdam because our mother was too sick to look after us. It was a strange story, because if our mother had been sick, we'd have been kept at home, since it was usual for girls of around ten years and older to take care of their mothers when they were sick. But the villagers were good people, not collaborators, and they never betrayed us.

About once every six months, my father's work colleague used to visit. She brought letters from my parents, who were in hiding separately from each other. First she came to see me and then my sister, who was with a different family in Sint Jacobiparochie. Then she went to Limburg, where my brothers were in hiding. She stayed only one night, so I had to write like crazy to answer their letters. I told my parents that I was doing the housekeeping, and later I wrote to them about cooking on an electric stove for the first time, and the way the milk boiled over if you left it alone for just a moment.

It's possible that the messenger also used to take care of the finances, because we had to pay for being in hiding. My father had already made preparations before the war. He had sold everything: furniture, piano, silver. I've always thought it was very clever of him to see what was coming and to take appropriate precautions.

In Friesland, the man who organized the addresses for people to go into hiding was a minister. One day, he came to the station. "I've been assigned to a parish in Bergum," he said. "It's some way

Lowina with one of her brothers and her sister, 1935

from here, to the east of Leeuwarden. You and your sister can come and live with us." It soon became clear that he needed help around the house. He had four children, the eldest of whom was four, and there was another on the way.

My sister was staying with a grocer and his family. She wasn't allowed to do anything, so the move might be a good thing for her. But what about me? "Well," I said to the minister, "I like being here, and they like having me. Perhaps you can find another girl."

"But your sister can go to school if you come with us to Bergum." That argument swayed me. My sister was twelve at the time, and it's important to go to school at that age. I hardly even thought about my own education. I was just happy that I'd been taken in by a fairly relaxed family, where I didn't have to be scared all the time of being caught and taken away.

I continued to resist, and he said, "If you don't come, the family won't get any more money or ration coupons." That's how it worked: With my fake identity card I got coupons that the family could use to buy food. Without those coupons, they could only buy food for their own family. And that wasn't very much. That didn't really matter to them, though. "You're welcome even without any coupons," they said. "If there's food for five, there's food for six."

But finally I agreed to go anyway. The house in Bergum was large, and so was the family. They put me to work immediately. My sister was allowed to go to school, which was good. We had to tell that unlikely story about our sick mother in Bergum too, as it was the minister who had come up with it, but once again no one betrayed us.

The minister often used to get so furious that he would throw his children from one end of the room to the other. His wife had no say in anything. She had a baby every year — and that was it. When he sat in his study on Saturday writing his sermon, we all had to be as quiet as mice, even the really little ones. I was used to discipline at home, but it was really extreme. I ran the household and, although I disliked the family, and I wasn't free to be myself, I still managed to fit in. I'd learned how to adapt by then. It had become second nature.

My sister was so nervous that she often used to wet the bed. Then the minister would shake her and hit her. And when he saw me watching, he used to lash out: "Oh yes, you're the queen, aren't you?" There was obviously something about my attitude or the look in my eyes that showed how much I loathed him. When she was in her fifties, my sister committed suicide. It must have been connected to all of the stress of our childhood.

At one point, some Germans were housed in the minister's home. They were there to build bunkers, not to track down Jewish people, but I was still terrified. They often used to come into the kitchen with some chickens or a rabbit. The maid and I would prepare it for them. But I refused to eat any of it: I didn't want to eat anything the Germans had caught or shot. The minister thought that was ridiculous. He couldn't stand my attitude. He said it would be dangerous for everyone if I refused to eat the food the Germans had brought. That was nonsense, of course. The Germans didn't eat with us, so there was no way they could see I wasn't eating their food.

I was so scared when we were living with the minister that I went to see a local doctor. I assumed that, like everyone else in Bergum, he was a good man, not a collaborator. I explained that my sister and I were sleeping in a garden room at the minister's house. "If the Germans ever raid the house," I said, "can we try to escape through the garden and come to you?" He said that would be fine. I was looking for a refuge, even though we still didn't have a clue what was happening to Jewish people in Germany and Poland. We thought you had to work very hard and they didn't give you enough to eat, so that if you died it was of natural causes. I wrote and told my father how scared I was in that house. Six months later he replied to say that I shouldn't be scared, but also that it made no sense not to eat their chickens. He said I shouldn't worry so much. That was a big disappointment. I wasn't able to talk to my sister about my visit to the doctor or about my fears. She was four years younger than me, after all. I felt so lonely.

Looking back, my fear was understandable. It wasn't my refusal to eat "German" food that put us at risk. The minister himself was the real danger. Every Sunday he preached from the pulpit about what had been said on **Radio Oranje**[40] that week, even though it was strictly forbidden to have a radio, let alone listen to Radio Oranje. And he talked about us, about the girls who were living in his house because of their sick mother.

It's hardly surprising that the minister and his family eventually had to go into hiding themselves. That meant that we had to leave too. My sister went with a teacher from Bergum to the island of Schiermonnikoog, where the woman had been born. She was going back to teach there. My sister had a good time on the island. The teacher, Aunt Martha, became a mother figure for her.

A woman from an organization that helped people to find hiding places took me on the back of her bike to a minister in Drachten. A month later, the same woman took me to stay with a young farming couple, where a Jewish boy was already in hiding. He was two or three years older than me, and his name was Bram. When the farmer went to bed, he would say, "Why don't the two of you stay here for a while?" On one of those evenings, I was introduced to sex. It was terrible. I didn't like the boy at all, but I did it anyway. I felt so guilty, particularly because I was still thinking about Jacques, the boy from the Jewish School. I knew he'd been deported and that it was by no means certain that he

---

40. **Radio Oranje:** radio station operated by the Dutch government in exile in London. Radio Oranje reported on the progress of the Allied forces, and Queen Wilhelmina gave a weekly radio address to lift the spirits of the people of the Netherlands.

was still alive, but I was ashamed because I had betrayed my own feelings. When it became dangerous to live with the young couple, I went to stay with an older farming couple in Jubbega. They had five children. The youngest, an unmarried daughter, still lived at home. Before the war, they'd been so poor that the farmer worked in Germany on weekdays. His wife was a sweet little old lady with a bent back. Summer and winter, she did the washing at four o'clock on Monday mornings, outside, on an old-fashioned washboard. They had never had much food, they had no comforts, and they had to work like dogs, but during that last winter of the war, when people from the west came knocking at the door to ask if there was anything to eat, they always had something to spare. They would shake their heads in amazement and say, "How is it that those city folk have no food?" They had a cow and a pig by then, so they were no longer as poor as they had once been.

Someone might knock at the door at any moment, and they were terrified that I would be discovered. "Go! Get out of sight!" they would shout when they saw anyone approaching in the distance. So in the daytime, I was only allowed to sit in the barn. It was a big, tall barn that they used for hay. I sat at a table by the door and I read. I left the door to the barn slightly open, for the fresh air, and to let in some light. I was allowed to stretch my legs a little in the evening, and I used to go for walks along the canal.

At night I shared the daughter's bed. She worked in a library and she brought home all kinds of books for me. So I sat there in that barn, reading books in German, English, and French. It seemed like a good idea, as I knew I'd have to go back to school at some point.

I stayed in Jubbega until the end of the war, and I even started putting on weight while I was there, because all I did was sit around. The place was never raided by the Germans, and I was able to control my fear. After the war though, it was so hard for me to cope that I didn't even think to thank the family. I still feel really bad about that. They're long dead by now of course, and their daughter's most likely passed away too.

I celebrated liberation in Friesland, in the town of IJlst, with Bram (the boy hidden at the farm) and his parents. The Germans had gone, which was wonderful, but I didn't have much to celebrate, and certainly not with Bram. I still went back to Amsterdam with him later though, to my old flat, which was empty. I was even engaged to him for a while, because our parents said we should.

I can't remember anything about my reunion with my parents and my brothers. My father asked for a divorce immediately after the war. When I heard, it was as though the floor beneath me cracked right open, like an earthquake. During the war, I thought that everything would be better later, at home and all over the world, and that we would all work together to build a new society. The divorce dashed all of those hopes. I felt completely alone. That feeling lasted for years.

In the years after the war, I became curious about all of my old classmates, particularly Jacques, but I was always too scared to try to find out what had happened to him. It wasn't until thirty years later that I went to the Hollandsche Schouwburg in Amsterdam, where the Jewish people who died in the war are commemorated on the walls. I discovered that Jacques had been gassed in Sobibor, almost immediately upon arrival.

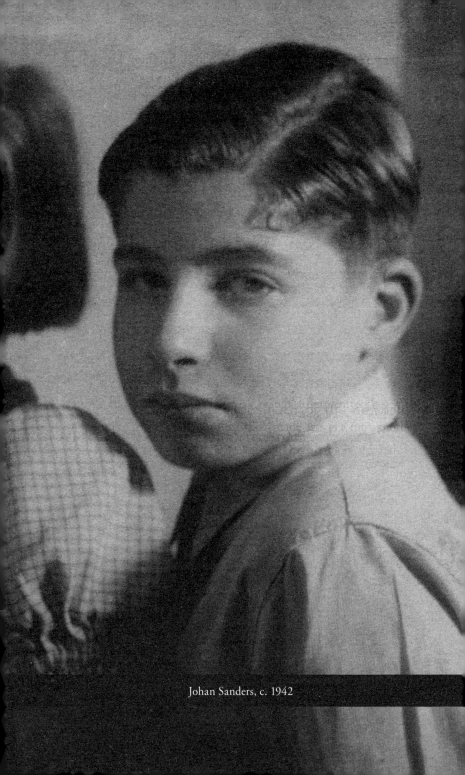

Johan Sanders, c. 1942

JOHAN VAN DE BERG'S IN LOVE WITH LENIE VISSERMAN!

JOHAN SANDERS
Born in Enschede, eastern Netherlands, August 6, 1931

When the war broke out, my father was visiting Paris on business. The weather was beautiful, a glorious summer's day. It was impossible to believe that there was a war on. As we had no telephone and nobody knew exactly what had happened to my father, the strangest rumors started making the rounds. People were saying, "Oh, Gerard Sanders, he's run away to Spain." But by May 14, we heard that he had made his way back to The Hague, having walked and hitched all the way from Paris. Escaping to Spain hadn't even occurred to him. He was too much of a family man. A few days later, he arrived back home in Enschede.

I come from an orthodox family, and we observed Jewish laws at home. My father was important to our whole family and community. His brothers, sisters, aunts, and uncles all saw him as a man you could rely on when you needed help or advice. On Shabbat we went to the synagogue and then our relatives would come back to our home or we would go visit them. We had to walk, because it was forbidden to ride a bike or drive a car on Shabbat. I never really enjoyed the thought of going to synagogue in the morning, followed by lunch with the family. "Just go," my mother used to say. "You'll look back on it fondly when you're older." It turned out that she was right. I miss those days even now.

The first major roundup in Enschede was on Sunday, September 14, 1941. We were warned in advance, and so my father was able to avoid capture. On that day, 105 young men from Enschede and the surrounding area were taken from their homes and imprisoned in the school gym. I saw them inside the building. I knew a few of the men, and I was able to pass on messages to some of the families and tell them that their father or their son was at the school.

The next day, all of the men were deported to Mauthausen concentration camp. The first reports of deaths came only two weeks later. One man was *"auf der Flucht erschossen"* (shot during an escape attempt), while another had caught typhus, and yet another had apparently died of pneumonia. In reality, they were forced to work themselves to death. Two months later, they were all dead. Every single one of them. We knew that because the Germans informed Sig Menko, the chairman of the Jewish Council in Enschede.

As a member of the council, my father went with the chairman to the monthly meetings of the Jewish Council in Amsterdam. At one meeting, Sig Menko stood up and said, "Gentlemen, we can give our people only one piece of advice: Go into hiding." The meeting was immediately suspended.

"We will not discuss that subject here," they said. "The words *go into hiding* are not part of our vocabulary."

So then Menko said to my father, "Sanders, come with me. We are leaving this meeting, and I will never return. You may come to Amsterdam as often as necessary, to observe. And that will be all. In Enschede we will do what we must, but we will resist whenever we can."

As my father worked for the Jewish Council, he was given a temporary exemption from deportation. Many of my father's acquaintances would come to Enschede on the train, walk to our house, which was near the station, come in through the front door, stay for two or three nights, and then disappear through the back door to an address where they went into hiding. It was all coordinated with Reverend Overduin's resistance group. I thought it was so exciting, a real adventure.

We were actually very curious to find out what would happen when we had to go into hiding ourselves. We knew that we'd have to live in some stranger's house and do as we were told and eat whatever food happened to be available. The food was sure not to be kosher, which is what we were accustomed to. By then, my sisters and I were the last Jewish children in Enschede. The others had all gone.

On the afternoon of Friday, April 9, 1943, the time finally came: We were taken to the home of a family of strangers. That evening someone collected us from the house. I stayed the night with the Overduin family and my sisters went with another family. The next morning we were all put on the train to Arnhem, about sixty miles to the west. My two sisters traveled in a different train car with the woman who was accompanying them, and I sat elsewhere in the train with a man. When we reached Arnhem, my sisters and I took the bus to another minister's home. We didn't stay there long: That afternoon I was told to take the bus to Veenendaal, twenty more miles to the west, where I was to stay with the Van Schuppen family, who owned a well-known cigar factory, Ritmeester Cigars.

When I went to bed that night, I found a sweater in my suitcase with a Jewish star on it. I tried to pull off the star, but there was no point. The fabric beneath it was much less faded than the rest of the sweater, so you could still see the outline of the star. We had to throw the sweater, star and all, into the fire.

During my stay with the Van Schuppens, I was brainwashed: I was no longer Johan Sanders but Johan van de Berg from Rotterdam, where I had lived on Mathenesserlaan. My mother had died during the bombing of Rotterdam, and my father was unable to take care of me.

On Monday evening, April 12, a Mr. Van Dijk came for my sisters. An hour later, Mr. Van Engelenburg came to fetch me and I went into hiding as Johan van de Berg. From one day to the next, I became part of a Christian family. The husband was a night porter at Ritmeester Cigars, where he worked until midnight. There was so much to get used to: my new family, the smell of the house, and the fact that I, an eleven-year-old, had to sleep beside a boy of five, when I'd never shared a bed with anyone before. Every day my foster parents made me play old maid and board games with the little boy, who was called Gert, until I'd had it up to here with old maid. I still detest games like that even now.

Although I was much older, Gert saw me as a playmate. He'd always been an only child, but now he had a big brother. In spite of our enforced relationship, we developed a strong bond, which is still intact even now.

I didn't look particularly Jewish, so I was allowed to go outside and play. The house was on a canal. There were all sorts of little boats on the water and it was great fun to rock around in them. The very first day, I went flying into the water. Headfirst into the duckweed! I had to go straight back home. All I

House in Veenendaal where Johan hid with the Van Engelenburg family

could say to my foster mother was, "Well, that's one way to dive into hiding!"

She just started laughing and said, "Johan, you shouldn't have gone on those boats, and you shouldn't have been rocking around in them." She treated me like her own son. Every week, she used to put a twenty-five-cent piece in my piggy bank and give me ten cents to buy candy.

After six months with the family, I found that I was covered in nasty sores. I felt really miserable, but I obviously couldn't go to the doctor. No one could understand how I'd gotten the sores, but they decided that they'd have to treat me themselves. First they made me eat yeast, which they got from the baker. That didn't do any good. Then my foster mother's sister — the only one outside the immediate family who knew I was Jewish — came up with an idea. The boy's never eaten pork in his entire life, she said. Perhaps he's allergic to it. So they stopped feeding me pork, and the sores went away.

The Van Engelenburg family took me everywhere with them, on visits to their relatives and even to church on Sundays. I went to a Christian school as well, where I had to memorize a psalm verse every week. In church, you always had your psalm book with you. And two peppermints to suck. That's where I first heard stories from the New Testament.

The family used to pray before eating, "Lord, bless this meal, amen." I had always worn a **keppel**[41] on my head during prayers. So instead, I used to cross my hands and cover my head. I was so used to doing it that it had become a habit. The family never noticed, because they had their eyes closed, but I would never have done it if there were strangers at the table.

My sisters, who were in hiding nearby, went to the same school as me. I saw them every day in the school yard, but I couldn't talk to them because no one was allowed to find out that they were my sisters. Whenever I had the chance, I used to give them the cards that I received from my teacher as a reward for reciting my weekly psalm without any mistakes. What was I going to do with them? I thought my sisters might like them. They were a lot younger than me.

Every day I walked to school with my foster brother. One time we saw my sisters on the street. We were walking in one

---

41. **keppel**: a skullcap, a small round head covering worn by religious Jewish men. Also called a kippah or yarmulke.

The street and canal facing the Van Engelenburgs' home, c. 1937

direction and they were going in the other. I was so happy that I couldn't stop myself. "You see those girls?" I blurted out to little Gert. "They're my sisters!" His eyes nearly popped out of his head. He never forgot what I'd told him, but he never revealed my secret. That was the only time I ever let my mouth run away with me.

We spent a lot of time playing out on the streets. I remember, when I was about twelve, I sometimes used to wink at my sisters. So there was at least a little contact between us. But once one of the boys laughed and said, "Ha-ha, Johan van de Berg's in love with Lenie Visserman!" Of course there was no way I could explain that Lenie was my sister.

I stayed with the Van Engelenburg family throughout most of the war, until the beginning of August 1944. One day, during vacation, we were out in the fields as usual, when a local farmer, Squint-Eyed Ot, came striding up to us. He was cursing away and said we'd been walking over his land and had let his chickens out.

We'd done nothing of the sort. Then he said to some other people, "That boy who's staying with Van Engelenburg, I'm going to make sure he gets taken away. He's not normal, if you know what I mean." In other words, he's Jewish.

That lunchtime, I found out that my foster mother's sister had already told them about the farmer's threat. They didn't want to run any risks, so they immediately went into action. After lunch, my foster father put me on the back of his bike and took me to the Van Schuppens so that they could find me another place to hide. That same evening, I went to stay with a childless married couple, where I became invisible for four or five weeks. I had to stay inside, and I spent whole days reading. But they couldn't borrow too many boys' books from the library, because people would have noticed. I learned how to clean vegetables and roll cigarettes when I was staying there. I spent a lot of time alone in my bedroom. I couldn't even stand at the window, because the people in the house next door were Nazi collaborators.

Fortunately, at the end of August, I was able to leave and go somewhere else, where I was allowed outside. It was a boarding house in Wageningen. I didn't realize at first, but I later found out that other Jewish people were hiding there too.

I clearly remember September 17, 1944, the day of the airborne landing at Arnhem.[42] We sat watching soldiers fall from the sky on the other side of the River Rhine, with weapons, bicycles,

---

42. airborne landing at Arnhem: British, Polish, and American soldiers parachuted down near Arnhem (a city in the eastern part of the Netherlands) in September 1944, but they didn't succeed in capturing the bridge over the Rhine at Arnhem, which meant that the northern part of the Netherlands still had to wait to be liberated.

and crates of ammunition. We thought the war was almost over then, but we were wrong. There was lots of serious fighting near Arnhem, and large numbers of people had to evacuate the area.

I was taken from the boarding house and ended up staying with Reverend Boer, a Protestant minister from Bennekom. Until the end of the war, I moved from place to place with him and his family. Of the couple's six children, only the eldest had survived: Jacob, a boy my age. He was extremely well behaved. One afternoon we raided the homemade plum jam supplies in the basement. Later, when his mother put the jam on the table, Jacob started crying.

"Jacob, why are you crying?" his mother asked.

"Johan and I have already eaten some," he sobbed. But fortunately she didn't punish us.

I had to play games with Jacob too. We usually played chess, and when I won, he went down into the basement to cry. We never became real friends, but I still had to share a bed with him. He always used to slide over to my side of the bed. One evening, I found a hatpin, and when he sprawled onto my half, I jabbed him with it. "Mommy, Mommy, Johan stabbed me," he yelled.

My first foster mother walked from Veenendaal to Renswoude a few times to visit me. One evening she arrived on the doorstep unexpectedly, and I was allowed to spend a few hours alone with her. I have such wonderful memories of that day; the two of us had formed a special bond.

When the Germans took over the rectory where we were living, we had to leave once again. As we traveled to our new temporary home, we saw more and more Germans trudging along with bowed heads, on their way back to their homeland. Soon after that, liberation came. Finally I could stop being scared.

A few days after liberation, my first foster father, Uncle Gert van Engelenburg, came up to me in the street. We'd kept in touch, and he knew where to find me.

"Johan, I've come to fetch you."

"To fetch me?"

"Yes, I have some news for you. Your mother's returned."

He lifted me onto the back of his bike and cycled to Veenendaal. As we approached the house, he gave me a nudge. "Look, here comes your mother."

She was older. I was older. We wanted to hug each other. I tried to hold her. She tried to hold me. But it felt very different from what I'd been dreaming about for so long. The two of us walked together to the house where my sisters were staying.

Some other people had moved into our house, which was next to the factory where my father had worked. They stayed there and it was October 1945 before we were given another house to rent. That was when we were really reunited as a family, but still missing my father. My sisters and I had gone into hiding on April 9, 1943, my mother on April 11, and my father on April 12 — a day too late. Apparently someone had betrayed him. Still we hoped for months after the war that he would return, that he might have escaped to Russia. That was until the Red Cross confirmed that his date of death had been registered as February 28, 1945. He was last seen in Gross-Rosen, a concentration camp in Poland.

We had nothing left and had to go looking for our furniture and the rest of our belongings. One day, Mother remembered that my father used to have a cow. During the war, he'd asked a farmer who worked at his factory to keep the cow in his barn in exchange for milk from the cow three times a week. My mother asked the farmer what had happened to the animal. "Oh, yes, that cow," he said. "It died. But what a pity your husband didn't come to stay on the farm himself, because then you'd still have him."

When my foster mother went into a nursing home many years later, Gert, my foster brother, had to clear out his parents' house. He asked me, "Is there anything you'd like to have as a keepsake?"

"Yes, there is," I answered, "but I don't dare ask."

"Ask away."

"The clock," I replied.

"Well," he said, "the clock's going to the home with my mother, but when she passes away, then it's yours."

She died a few years later. After the funeral we went back to the nursing home for a bite to eat and a cup of coffee. Gert went to her room, took the clock from the wall, and handed it to me.

The clock used to hang in the living room of the house in

Veenendaal where I spent most of my months in hiding. I slept in the room above, and I could hear it through the floor. The sound of ticking used to make me feel safe. And now that clock serves as a permanent reminder of the darkest days of my life.

Donald, January 1940, just before the war

YEARS OF TEARS

DONALD DE MARCAS
Born in Leiden, June 29, 1933

All of my grandparents died long before the war. Fortunately they didn't have to live through it. My mother's father was a dealer in rags, metals, and animal hides. My grandfather De Marcas had a cake bakery in Zwolle. My father didn't like baking, so he went to Germany to learn about the men's fashion industry instead. He took over a clothing store in Leiden around 1930.

There was such warmth in our family home. My mother raised me so gently. We cuddled a lot. My mother was a very small woman, which had made the birth difficult, and so I remained an only child. She often used to sing to me and accompany herself on the piano. She would sing me to sleep while I made little noises in my crib. I wanted to join in with the singing.

I wasn't as close to my father. I hardly ever went to the store, and when I played there I had to keep quiet. That was difficult, because I was a chatterbox. It was an elegant store and his customers included the mayor and the city council of Leiden and professors from the university. "That lady laughs just like a goat," I once said about a customer. My father immediately dragged me out to the back of the store.

The store stayed open in the summer months, so my father and mother always took separate vacations, and I used to stay with a friend of my mother's, where I suddenly had a new brother and sister and two lovely dogs, boxers. I always enjoyed going there.

I remember the atmosphere just before the war. It was very threatening. My parents often used to go with friends to Noordwijk. They sat there talking, outside a bar by the sea. It was 1939. I didn't understand what they were talking about — I wasn't even six at the time — but I could feel the worry, the fear.

My bedroom in Leiden was next to my parents' room. There was a small window in the door between our rooms, and I could hear them through it as they discussed the news on the radio on the morning war broke out. The war made me aware for the first time that people felt Jews were different. The war is what made me Jewish.

I felt the full force of the threat when my father had to close down his business. Soon after that we had to leave our big house on the Botermarkt in the center of town and we moved in with the Moks, another Jewish family in Leiden. They had a small garden, where I was allowed to grow marigolds and cress.

During that time, we tried once to go into hiding, with a carpenter. My parents used to call him Mr. Wood Glue. We camped out in his badly lit attic. Within two weeks, my parents

The Jewish school Pieterskerkhof in Leiden, 1943. Donald is the second from the right.

couldn't put up with it any longer, and we went back to the Mok family.

One night my mother woke me up. There was an NSB member standing in the doorway to my bedroom. They took us from our beds and drove us to the police station in Leiden, where we found lots of Jewish friends and acquaintances. Then we went to Hollands Spoor station in The Hague, where the train to Westerbork was waiting for us.

We were fortunate that my father had been persuaded to set up a Jewish Council in Leiden a few months before, in the hope of helping his fellow Jews. When we were standing on the platform, he said, "Don't get on that train. I'm going to look for the man in charge." The man's name was Fischer. They called him *Judenfischer*, the Jew Fisher, because of the way he went after Jewish people.

"I'm the head of the Jewish Council in Leiden," said my father. "I need to return to my post."

"Ihr Gesicht gefällt mir nicht," (I don't like your face) said Fischer, who had had a drink or two. But still the train left without us.

Now we knew we had to go into hiding. "You can go to my brother, Meindert Zaalberg," said Aunt Truus, a woman who sang in the same choir as my mother. But Aunt Truus had to work hard to bring my parents around. They didn't want to go into hiding. My father was convinced he could still help other people. Finally they agreed, and we took our suitcases and went with Uncle Meindert to his pottery in Leiderdorp.

Uncle Meindert was in the resistance. They did target practice at his place and would shoot at the piles of peat that he used to fire the pottery kilns. My parents had two small rooms upstairs in their house, which was next door.

One evening Uncle Meindert came and sang to us and accompanied himself on the guitar. He sang Dutch words to the tune of "Hatikvah," which later became Israel's national anthem. I had never heard the tune before, and I found it very moving.

Uncle Meindert was a passionate and religious man. "We have a wall around our house," he said, "and no one will get through it." There was such strength in the way he said it. I really admired him. In spite of his belief that we would be safe, he was still very aware of any threats. When he heard rumors that there was going to be a raid in our neighborhood, he took Father and Mother to his summer cottage in Noordwijkerhout. Uncle Meindert was right: There was a raid, but they stopped at our neighbors' house.

I had already left by then. Uncle Meindert thought it was better to split up the family, so that if there was a raid, they wouldn't get us all at the same time.

My first address was with Reverend Dijk, also in Leiderdorp. I used to go back to stay with that family whenever I needed another change of address. After I'd been there for a few weeks, Uncle Meindert arranged for me to stay in Breda with the wife of a high-up military man who was a prisoner of war in Poland. She gave me a warm welcome, but her children found it more difficult. What kind of strange boy had come to their house? And why wasn't he allowed outside?

From my room, a beautiful front room on the first floor, I could look out onto the street. Some children were playing hide-and-seek, and others were jumping rope. I felt so homesick, and I wrote long letters to my parents. Uncle Slothouwer, our contact person in the resistance, used to deliver them for me.

Later I went to stay with the Marijnissen family, who lived close to the Belgian border. Uncle Toon Marijnissen was a game-keeper who was in charge of a large estate. Aunt Net and Uncle Toon had one child, little Jantje, and a dog, Max. Uncle Toon hunted poachers, but he did just as much poaching himself. We ate lots of rabbits and hares. Although I didn't look typically Jewish, Aunt Net thought it was a good idea to bleach my hair. She did it in the kitchen. I had to stand on a stool and hang my head in a bowl, while Aunt Net soaped me up. We waited for the stuff she rubbed into my hair to soak in. Then she rinsed it out under the pump and I had light-brown hair.

Donald with the Marijnissen family, 1943

I also had chores to do. Every two days, I had to walk over a mile with a jug to a neighboring farmer to fetch milk. The farmer had two daughters, who were very fond of me. They gave me all kinds of good things to eat. Another of my jobs was picking grass for the rabbits every day in the field behind our house.

Uncle Toon and Aunt Net had lots of friends. They used to have card game evenings, and people would wander in and out of the house. It had been drummed into me that I wasn't allowed to talk about where I came from. But their close friends must have known I wasn't a family relative but a little boy who was in hiding.

I slept in an attic room with a small window. When there was a storm and I was scared, I was allowed to sleep in between Aunt Net and Uncle Toon. I had a good life there, although I missed my mom and dad. We wrote long letters to each other, but nothing remains of them now. We had to burn them or tear them up after reading them.

Unfortunately I had to leave that place. There was a very talkative priest in the village and he liked to chat with me — and with everyone else. After ten months there, Uncle Toon and Aunt Net, who were closely involved with the resistance, thought it would be safer for me to move to a new address.

Uncle Slothouwer picked me up and took me back to Reverend Dijk in Leiderdorp. Before eating, I used to make the sign of the cross. I'd picked up that Catholic habit from the family I'd been staying with. It made the family laugh. A little Jewish boy sitting at the dinner table with a Protestant minister and crossing himself before eating!

Usually I slept in a bedroom with the eldest son, but one night I was allowed to have the room to myself. Late that evening, two shadowy figures appeared in the darkened room: It was my parents. They were still hiding at the nearby potter's workshop. They'd come to visit me, and the minister had made sure that we'd be alone.

"Hello, Auntie." That's what I said to my mother. It was how I'd been taught to greet any woman who came to visit. My mother was really sad that I didn't recognize her immediately, but she didn't let it show. We sat and talked in the dimly lit room. I can't remember if we had a cuddle, but I do remember saying good-bye. Then they went back to their own hiding place.

A few weeks later, I went to stay at the boys' orphanage that was run by the friars in Tilburg. I took the name of Jan van den Heuvel, after the square in the center of Tilburg, De Heuvel (the hill). There were three other children in hiding among the forty orphans: one Jewish boy and two brothers whose father was in the resistance.

Monastery and orphanage where Donald stayed in Tilburg

Next to the boys' orphanage was the monastery, where the friars lived. Most of the forty men worked as teachers, and three of them were responsible for running the orphanage. Although we were posing as orphans, the friars knew that we were in hiding.

Occasionally, one of the orphans would notice that I was different. "Why does Jan never take communion?" one of them once asked. Another one said, "Why does Jan never have to confess?" You had to be Catholic to go to communion and confession.

I went to church so often that I knew exactly how the services went, and I always noticed when one of the altar boys made a mistake. I prayed and begged to be allowed to become an altar boy. I loved the drama of it all. But you had to be baptized to be an altar boy.

Otherwise, I joined in with daily life at the orphanage, just like everyone else. I helped to set the long tables, ate with the others, played with them, and went on vacation with them to Veghel. I didn't want to stand out, so I became very good at fitting in.

There was just one radio in the orphanage. I often used to listen to the radio with Brother Gaudentius, the head of the orphanage, especially after October 1944, when Tilburg was liberated. We used to sit in his room. Brother Gaudentius was a rather plump and messy man. He always smoked cigars, and the ash used to fall down onto his stained habit.

I listened so eagerly to that radio. We'd been liberated, but the rest of the country was still under German occupation. We heard about a famine, about a Hunger Winter. What did that mean for my parents? Sitting there in that room with Brother Gaudentius, I was very aware of the war. But I didn't talk about it

The four hidden boys at the orphanage in Tilburg (Donald is on the right), 1944

with my friends at the orphanage. Ever. Those months were terrible. I remember feeling so insecure and how frustrating it was that I couldn't be with my parents even though we'd already been liberated.

After liberation, life in the orphanage changed completely. Some British soldiers were housed in the monastery. We celebrated Christmas with them, and for the first time in my life I ate plum pudding. We also learned English songs, which I really loved.

My time in hiding didn't come to an end until the rest of the Netherlands was also liberated, on May 5, 1945.

It was another month and a half before my father came for me. Strangely, I can't remember anything about our reunion. Or about the journey back to Leiden on the train. Or about seeing my mother again. I do remember that we weren't allowed to go back to our own house at number 17, Botermarkt. It had to be vacated. And fumigated. While we waited for that to happen, we stayed with a cousin of my mother's. We listened to the radio at her place, to the people from the Red Cross reading out lists of Jewish people who had been murdered. It turned out that all of our relatives except for two cousins had been killed. What followed was years of tears. A whole lifetime. That war will not be over until I take my last breath.

It wasn't easy to rebuild my relationship with my parents. I'd been responsible for myself for so long that I found it hard to have parents who wanted to be involved in my life. Discovering that their entire family had been massacred also created a distance between us. They were locked away in their grief. They had to work really hard to get the store up and running too. That was no easy task: My father was fifty-six, and the business had been completely ruined. Even the wood paneling had been burned as firewood.

In the fall of 1945, he opened the doors again and many of his former clients returned. Other customers said, "Mr. De Marcas, we're sorry, but your competitor was so helpful during the war. We think it's the right thing for us to stay with him."

Father was able to deal with the pain better than Mother, who was never as affectionate as she had been before the war. She was troubled by nightmares for years. She used to dream about the concentration camp where her only sister was murdered along with her husband and children. The war destroyed the mother I had known.

THE HIDDEN

CHILDREN

TODAY

Rita Prins-Degen   Jaap Sitters

Bloeme Evers-Emden

Jack Eljon

Rose-Mary Weijel-Kahn

Lies Lisser-Elion (1931–2011)

Maurice Meijer   Leni Meijer-de Vries

Harry and Sieny Cohen

Benjamin Kosses   Michel Goldsteen

Lowina de Levie   Johan Sanders

Donald de Marcas

GLOSSARY

Allies: the countries that fought together against the Germans in World War II, which included Canada, France, Poland, the Soviet Union, the United Kingdom, and the United States.

Arbeitseinsatz (German: forced labor): Many German men had been called up to join the army, so Dutch men were taken to Germany to work there toward the end of the war. The men, and sometimes women, were simply rounded up and sent to Germany. Many non-Jewish men tried to escape this forced labor by going into hiding like the Jews.

"auf der Flucht erschossen": In German, "shot during an escape attempt," a common phrase used to explain a prisoner's cause of death.

concentration camp: a large prison camp where people were treated very badly and often died from malnutrition, abuse, or serious illnesses. In many concentration camps, people were murdered, often upon arrival. These camps were known as extermination camps. Two of the best-known camps are Auschwitz-Birkenau and Sobibor. Most of the Dutch Jews were murdered in these two camps.

curfew: the time in the evening by which everyone had to be off the streets.

Dolle Dinsdag (Dutch: Mad Tuesday): Tuesday September 5, 1944. The Belgian cities of Antwerp and Brussels had been liberated two days before, and the Dutch thought they would soon be liberated as well. Everyone was mad with happiness. However, it was not until May 5, 1945, that the Netherlands was finally liberated.

Frisian, or **West Frisian**: a language closely related to Dutch, which is spoken in the province of Friesland in the north of the Netherlands.

front line: in a war zone, the area where fighting is taking place.

Gestapo: the German secret police. Their main activity was tracking down the enemies of the German occupiers. The Gestapo then sent their "enemies" to concentration camps with no legal representation. They were known for torturing their prisoners.

Hollandsche Schouwburg: a theater in Amsterdam that the German occupiers used between August 1942 and November 1943 to imprison Jews before they were sent to concentration camps. Young children of families held there were taken to a kindergarten across the street.

Hunger Winter (Dutch: *Hongerwinter*): the Dutch famine in winter 1944–45, when there was a serious shortage of food in much of the Netherlands, causing many people to starve to death.

Jewish Council (German: *Judenrat*): administrative organizations that the German occupiers ordered Jewish communities to set up to manage Jewish affairs. The council had the task of carrying out some of the measures that the Germans imposed on the Jews. Anyone who worked for the Jewish Council was temporarily exempted from deportation. Thousands of people were involved in the work of these organizations.

Many Jewish people resented the council members, particularly the leaders, for following the orders of the occupying Germans, and they thought the exemption from deportation was unfair, but a lot of Jewish Council members secretly tried to help others whenever they had the chance.

keppel: a skullcap, a small round head covering worn by religious Jewish men. Also called a kippah or yarmulke.

mixed marriage: usually a marriage between two people of different religious backgrounds or nationalities. In this case, a marriage between a Jew and a non-Jew. Generally, Jews in mixed marriages were not required to report for deportation, and their children did not have to wear stars on their clothing to indicate that they were Jewish. They did, however, have to obey the other rules that the German occupiers had made for Jews.

NSB, or *Nationaal-Socialistische Beweging*: the National Socialist Movement, a kind of political party in the Netherlands (1931–45), which was modeled on Adolf Hitler's Nazi Party in Germany. The NSB often worked with the German occupiers.

Piet Meerburg's group: a resistance group that arranged safe houses for Jewish children. The group managed to hide about 350 Jewish children between 1942 and 1945.

PRA, or *Politieke Recherche Afdeling*: Political Investigation Department, set up after the war to serve justice on Dutch people who had collaborated with the Germans.

Pulsing: clearing out a home of all its possessions; the name comes from Abraham Puls, who the Germans had given the job of emptying out the homes of Jews who had gone into hiding or who had been taken away during a raid.

race laws: three racist, anti-Jewish laws that Germany introduced on September 15, 1935, which meant that Jewish citizens no longer had any civil rights. These laws were later responsible for Jews being systematically persecuted and murdered.

Radio Oranje: Radio Orange, a radio station operated by the Dutch government in exile in London. Radio Oranje reported on the progress of the Allied forces, and Queen Wilhelmina gave a weekly radio address to lift the spirits of the people of the Netherlands.

raid: a police or army action to find people and take them into custody.

requisitioned: claimed by the government or the authorities for their use, particularly for military purposes.

the resistance: organizations carrying out activities against occupying forces, such as helping people go into hiding, printing and distributing underground newspapers, and acts of sabotage.

Schutzstaffel, or **SS**: a paramilitary organization often seen as the most brutal division of Adolf Hitler's Nazi Party. Initial responsibility of the SS was protecting Hitler and his party members, but later extended to include enforcement of racial laws. Made up of several divisions, including the Gestapo and SD.

Shabbat: the Jewish day of rest. Shabbat runs from a few minutes before sunset on Friday until the appearance of three stars in the sky on

Saturday evening and is intended as a day of rest to honor God and the creation of the heavens and the earth.

shul: a Jewish place of worship where people come together to pray and learn. The word *shul* comes from Yiddish (the language of the Jews of eastern Europe) and is related to the German word *Schule* (school). *Shul* is another word for synagogue.

Sicherheitsdienst, or **SD**: German intelligence unit of SS, known for interrogating and torturing prisoners.

Sperre (German: block): a stamp in a person's identity card that exempted them from transportation to a concentration camp. The Germans could withdraw the *Sperre* at any moment, which eventually happened in almost every case.

star: a Star of David on a yellow background with the word *Jood* (Dutch: Jew) in the center. From May 3, 1942, all Jews six years and older had to wear this star on their outer clothes. The star had to be clearly visible and firmly attached, or the person would be punished.

Talmud: a central book of Judaism, containing rabbis' commentaries on the Jewish bible (Torah) as well as Jewish law.

Wehrmacht: the name of the German army from 1935 to 1945.

Westerbork: Before the war, Westerbork was established by the Dutch government as an internment camp for German-Jewish refugees. This changed during the war, when the Germans turned Westerbork into a transit camp. Almost all of the Jews who were rounded up in the Netherlands were sent by train to Westerbork, where they were kept in very primitive conditions. Mainly Jews, but also other groups of "undesirable aliens," were sent first to Westerbork and then to the concentration and extermination camps. Between July 15, 1942, and September 13, 1944, ninety-three trains headed to the east, carrying 102,000 Jews. Around 5,000 Jews returned to the Netherlands after liberation.

Yad Vashem medal: an Israeli medal to honor non-Jews who risked their lives to help Jews during the Holocaust.

ACKNOWLEDGMENTS

This book would not exist without the participation of the people who shared their stories with us. It was not only difficult at times for the contributors themselves to recall the past, but some of these stories also stirred up painful memories for their partners. We are most grateful to all of the following people: Harry Cohen, Sieny Cohen-Kattenburg, Jack Eljon, Betty Eljon-Peperwortel, Bloeme Evers-Emden, Michel Goldsteen, Didje Goldsteen-Uijterschout, Bennie Kosses, Lammie Kosses-Drenth, Lowina de Levie, Jacques Lisser, Lies Lisser-Elion, Donald de Marcas, Sonja de Marcas-Bernd't, Maurice Meijer, Leni Meijer-de Vries, Marja Minderman van Driessel, Ad Prins, Rita Prins-Degen, Johan Sanders, Jaap Sitters, Carla Sitters-van der Horst, Arnold Weijel, and Rose-Mary Weijel-Kahn.

And thanks, of course, to the organizations that made this project possible: the Stichting Collectieve Maror-gelden Nederland, the Mediafonds, the Nederland Fonds voor de Film, the Mondriaanstichting, and the Stichting Christelijke Pers. And to De Joodse Omroep for their confidence and support, both moral and financial, right from the very beginning of this project.

We gratefully made use of Jaap Sitters's book, *Jelle*, for the chapter "Three Pianos," and of Bloeme Evers-Emden's notes for the chapter "I'll Go Fetch Her Tomorrow Morning." In one story, a name has been changed at the interviewee's request.

Marcel Prins was inspired to create this project by his mother, who went into hiding in 1942 to escape Nazi persecution. She was just six years old at the time. Mr. Prins is an award-winning documentary filmmaker and cameraman. He lives in Utrecht, the Netherlands.

Peter Henk Steenhuis is a journalist who lives and works in Amsterdam, the Netherlands.

Laura Watkinson is a literary translator, and has three times been the recipient of the Batchelder Award for her translations from Dutch into English. She lives in Amsterdam, the Netherlands.

For more stories, photos, and information, visit
www.hiddenlikeannefrank.com.

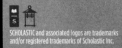